MANAGING EDUCATIONAL INNOVATIONS

WITHDRAWN

Unwin Education Books

Managing Educational Innovations

AUDREY NICHOLLS
Faculty of Education, Ulster Polytechnic

London
GEORGE ALLEN & UNWIN
Boston   Sydney

George Allen & Unwin (Publishers) Ltd,
40 Museum Street, London WC1A 1LU, UK

George Allen & Unwin (Publishers) Ltd,
Park Lane, Hemel Hempstead, Herts HP2 4TE, UK

Allen & Unwin, Inc.,
9 Winchester Terrace, Winchester, Mass. 01890, USA

George Allen & Unwin Australia Pty Ltd,
8 Napier Street, North Sydney, NSW 2060, Australia

First published in 1983

British Library Cataloguing in Publication Data

Nicholls, Audrey
    Managing educational innovations. – (Unwin education books)
1. Educational innovations
I. Title
370   LB1027
ISBN 0-04-370145-0
ISBN 0-04-370146-9 Pbk

Library of Congress Cataloging in Publication Data

Nicholls, Audrey.
    Managing educational innovations.
    (Unwin education books)
Includes bibliographical references and index.
1. Educational innovations. I. Title. II. Series.
LB1027.N335   1983   370′.7′33   83-8785
ISBN 0-04-370145-0
ISBN 0-04-370146-9 (pbk.)

Set in 10 on 11 point Times by Computape (Pickering) Ltd
and printed in Great Britain
by Billing and Sons Ltd, London and Worcester

Contents

With love to Laura, my granddaughter

Chapter 1

Innovation: Some Issues and Problems

To manage innovations effectively implies elements of planning, control, direction and order. Management has been analysed as involving the activities of planning, regulating, commanding, co-ordinating, controlling and evaluating (Urwick, 1963). The alternative to effective management of innovation is likely to result in a waste of time, money and effort and the possibility of a poorer quality of education because the desired improvement does not become a reality. Clearly, at a time of severe financial restrictions, when the most efficient use of human and material resources is essential, and at a time of increased concern about the quality of education, it becomes particularly important that those wishing to introduce educational innovations should do so as effectively as possible.

There is some evidence to suggest that attempts by teachers to innovate have not always been successful, in spite of considerable innovative activity (Gross *et al.*, 1971; Schmuck and Miles, 1971; Smith and Keith, 1971; Bealing, 1972; Tomlinson, 1978; Nicholls, 1979). Lack of success has been seen variously as failure to implement innovations, innovation without change and the replacement of one rigid and static practice by another. Observers offer several reasons for this state of affairs. Some believe that knowledge of planned organisational change is limited (Miles, 1964a; Bennis, 1966; CERI, 1973); others believe that there is insufficient knowledge of the implementation of innovations (Hoyle, 1970; Gross *et al.*, 1971); some argue that it is lack of attention to what *is* known about the processes of innovation that results in failure (Guba, 1968; McLaughlin, 1976; Nicholls, 1979).

The purpose of this book is to present knowledge and ideas about innovation drawn from several disciplines and fields of study, and to suggest how these might be applied to educational innovations, in the hope that readers might draw from it what seems relevant to their own situation. In such a complex enterprise as the promotion of educational innovation, which is so much influenced by its own particular setting and by the participants, no guarantees of success or even do-it-yourself manuals can be offered. However, what can be offered is a body of relevant knowledge and examples of previous experience which can provide the educational innovator with a more secure theoretical and practical background on which to base his decisions.

WHAT IS INNOVATION?

In everyday usage the words change and innovation are frequently used interchangeably and while this is also to be found in the literature a clear distinction between the two is also made. For example, innovation is seen as being something which is essentially new rather than a re-ordering of something which already exists into a new pattern; change calls for a response but innovation requires initiative (Owen, 1973). In the context of education this notion of innovation seems somewhat strict, especially in the light of the commonly held view that there is nothing really new in education. A more lenient view, while acknowledging that the terms change and innovation are used synonymously in schools, makes a distinction between the two and suggests that it would be incorrect to regard every change as an innovation. According to this view, an innovation must imply an improvement towards a predetermined objective and always presupposes one or more qualitative criteria (Marklund, 1972).

The literature abounds with varied and sometimes conflicting definitions of innovation, but there appears to be general agreement about three aspects: first, that it is fundamental in nature; secondly, that it is deliberate and planned; and thirdly that there is the intention of improvement. One definition, for instance, emphasises the fundamental nature of innovation when it states that any major innovation implies a change in the culture of the school so that 'authority relationships, communication networks, status groupings, and even friendship cliques are forced to change' if the innovation is to survive (Schmuck, 1974, p. 108).

In a frequently quoted definition deliberate planning and the improvement of performance are emphasised as characteristics of an innovation:

> Generally speaking, it seems useful to define an innovation as a deliberate, novel, specific change which is thought to be more efficacious in accomplishing the goals of a system ... it seems helpful to consider innovations as being planned for, rather than as occurring haphazardly. The element of novelty, implying recombination of parts or a qualitative difference from existing forms, seems quite essential. (Miles, 1964a, p. 14)

Similarly, another definition regards innovation as a 'deliberate attempt to improve practice in relation to certain desired objectives'

(CERI, 1973, p. 36), while an earlier study offers a similar but lengthier definition:

> We understand innovation to mean those attempts at change in an educational system which are consciously and purposefully directed with the aim of improving the present system. Innovation is not necessarily something new but it is something better and can be demonstrated as such. (CERI, 1969, p. 13)

The emphasis on the qualitative aspects of innovation implies that an innovation is not introduced simply for its own sake, and this point is made explicitly in another definition:

> by innovation we mean any change in one component of the educational system which is not made simply for the sake of change but with the intention of promoting improvements in the aspect concerned and – having regard to the close interdependence of all such aspects – in the system as a whole. (Noel, 1974, p. 29)

While there is a good measure of agreement about the fundamental, deliberate and improvement aspects of innovations, there is less agreement about their uniqueness, as some of the definitions already quoted indicate. The CERI (1969) definition says that an innovation is not necessarily something new and Miles refers to a recombination of parts, while Owen rejects the notion that an innovation can be merely a rearrangement of old constituent parts and looks for essential newness. A significant contribution to this debate is made by Rogers and Shoemaker (1971):

> An innovation is an idea, practice or object perceived as new by an individual. It matters little so far as human behaviour is concerned, whether or not an idea is 'objectively' new as measured by the lapse of time since its first use or discovery. It is the perceived or subjective newness of the idea for the individual that determines his reaction to it. If the idea seems new to the individual, it is an innovation. (p. 19)

This observation is about innovations in all fields, but it is particularly relevant to educational innovations which frequently require teachers to change attitudes, relationships and roles. There would appear to be no shortage of educational innovations and it is the implementation rather than the creation which presents certain difficulties and problems; and these will operate just as much if the idea or practice is new only to the individuals concerned or is 'objectively' new.

This leads to the view of innovation which will be taken in this book; it brings together elements of some of the definitions quoted earlier. An innovation is an idea, object, or practice perceived as new by an individual or individuals, which is intended to bring about improvement in relation to desired objectives, which is fundamental in nature and which is planned and deliberate. Innovation, as just defined, is the concern of this book, rather than *change* which is seen as a continuous reappraisal and improvement of existing practice and which can be regarded as part of the normal activity of curriculum development. However, the word change is occasionally used, for instance, in references from other writers and in widely used phrases such as 'planned organisational change' or 'processes of change'.

DIFFICULTIES ASSOCIATED WITH INNOVATION

It is difficult to bring about educational innovation, as earlier references to lack of success have suggested. It has already been mentioned that some writers see lack of knowledge or a disregard of knowledge of planning processes as a problem. However, this is not the only difficulty or problem associated with innovation; some other difficulties will be considered briefly here while possible solutions will be discussed later.

By definition, innovation is fundamental in nature and many educational innovations necessitate considerable changes in teachers' attitudes. Some involve teachers in changing their traditional roles and bring about new kinds of relationships both among teachers and between teachers and their pupils. Team-teaching is an example of such an innovation. Involvement in team-teaching could mean, for instance, among other changes, that a teacher would move from the privacy of a self-contained classroom to teaching in the presence of colleagues, from planning individually to planning jointly with colleagues, from teaching groups of, say, thirty pupils to working with groups of varying sizes up to as many as a hundred pupils. Not all teachers can make such changes in behaviour easily, even if they are willing to try.

Related to this is the fact that an innovation frequently requires teachers to give up practices in which they feel secure and display high levels of competence and to adopt new practices in which, at least temporarily, they feel less secure and in which they might possibly be less competent. There are expectations that teachers should be competent, and some may not be willing or able to tolerate even a temporary incompetence or to tolerate feelings of insecurity.

The extra workload that innovation brings should not be overlooked. The tasks of planning and implementing innovations bring work in addition to the normal teaching duties of teachers. Some teachers find participation in innovation so stimulating and exciting that they willingly accept the extra work; others might accept the extra work for other reasons: they might, for instance, see involvement in innovation as a way to promotion. There are other teachers, however, less enthusiastic about innovation or perhaps deriving their professional satisfaction from their classroom activities, who are much less willing to take on the additional task of innovating.

Closely related to the extra workload is the time factor. There are two aspects of this: time needed during the working week for planning and the period of time over which planning needs to be carried out. The tasks involved in the planning and implementation of innovations are time-consuming in both the dimensions mentioned, although it is the first which teachers often highlight as a problem. It is said that it is difficult to find time during the week when teachers can come together for planning purposes. Undoubtedly there are problems in this respect, but teachers in some schools find ways of overcoming the problems, either through skilful timetabling arrangements or by meeting after school (Evans and Groarke, 1975; Holt, 1976; Prosser, 1976; Nicholls, 1979). The long-term nature of planning and implementation is less frequently identified by teachers as a problem. Rather, they tend to underestimate the time needed. Innovators are frequently impatient and want to see their ideas put into practice quickly and this can result in the ideas being insufficiently examined and discussed; the final consequence of such impatience is partial or inadequate implementation.

The cost of innovation is often cited as a difficulty. It is a fact that some educational innovations are expensive. This would be true of those innovations that involve new materials or equipment. However, even in the case of such innovations it may be pertinent to ask not only whether the innovation is going to be costly, but whether it is going to be *more costly* than that which it is to replace. Not all innovations necessitate expensive equipment or materials and it would be most unfortunate if teachers were to think that the present economic restrictions of necessity preclude innovation. Indeed, one can envisage how economic difficulties might actually generate innovation. For instance, a secondary school which is unable to replace teachers who leave might have to implement significant curriculum and organisational innovations.

One factor which sometimes makes it difficult to persuade teachers to become involved in innovation is the difficulty of showing that the innovation will be more successful than present practice. The definition of innovation proposed earlier includes the words 'intended to bring about improvement'. The problem, common enough in education, is how to show that there is improvement. The difficulties surrounding evaluation in education have frequently led to a situation in which teachers involved in innovation have ignored any evaluation of them. It has been suggested elsewhere (Nicholls and Nicholls, 1975) that any new curriculum can be no more than a hypothesis to be tested for whether it will lead to the achievement of desired ends. However difficult it may be, criteria for the evaluation of an innovation should be included as an essential element. No guarantees can be given that the innovation will prove to be effective, but at least there will be some evidence on which to base decisions about its future.

CONSEQUENCES OF FAILURE TO INNOVATE

Given that there are so many problems and difficulties associated with innovation it seems reasonable that teachers may ask why they should innovate. It has become almost a platitude to state that we live not only in a period of rapid social change but also in a period in which the rate of change is still increasing. As institutions established by society, schools are affected by changes in society, and, to some extent at least, what takes place in schools has an influence on certain aspects of society. If society is changing significantly, then it can reasonably be expected that schools, as institutions of society, should also change significantly. This is not to suggest, however, that schools should respond indiscriminately to pressures emanating from other elements of society. Any response should be deliberate and planned and based on an explicit well-thought-out rationale so that decisions made can be defended and justified (Walton and Welton, 1976; Nicholls and Nicholls, 1978).

Not all changes in society may be considered by teachers to be desirable. Indeed, teachers are sometimes expected by the general public to redress some of these changes manifested by young people: changed attitudes to authority, vandalism and hooliganism. Teachers probably have insufficient power or influence to put to rights the ills of society, however willing they may be to try. The problem of teachers having different values from the rest of society is very difficult to cope with. Up to a certain point it might be considered desirable for teachers to display some idealism through what they are trying to achieve, but there are dangers in moving too far from reality. The discrepancy between teachers' views of school objectives and subjects and those of 15-year-old pupils and their parents was revealed in a government survey (Schools Council, 1968).

If the gap between the values and attitudes of teachers in school and those of the rest of society, particularly pupils, becomes too great, then schools are likely to be ineffective in carrying out their purposes. Pupils are likely to become apathetic, alienated and perhaps disruptive and in these circumstances desired learning will not take place. It is well known that there are schools that have large numbers of such pupils and while it would be unfair and untrue to suggest that this behaviour is the result of the schools' unwillingness to innovate, it might be considered prudent for all teachers to examine rigorously the curriculum, organisational arrangements, relationships, attitudes and values that operate in their schools.

THE RATE OF INNOVATION

If mature adult members of the general public were to visit schools they would find them very little changed in fundamental ways from when they themselves were pupils. Several writers comment on the slow rate of change in the field of education. Much of the early work in this area was carried out in the United States and one of the earliest writers to comment on the slow rate was Ross (1958) whose observations on a 150 studies were later substantiated by Mort (1964). These early studies indicated that in the American school system innovation went through a very slow process and followed a predictable pattern. There was typically a period of fifty years between insight into a need and the introduction of a way of meeting that need that was destined for general acceptance. Another fifty years was then required for the diffusion of the innovation. Mort says:

> during that half-century of diffusion, the practice is not recognised until it has appeared in three per cent of the systems of the country. By that time, fifteen years of diffusion – or independent innovation – have elapsed. Thereafter, there is a rapid twenty years of diffusion, accompanied by much fanfare, and then a long period of slow diffusion through the last small percentage of school systems. (p. 318)

Mort goes on to state that this slow rate can be speeded up under certain circumstances, namely, when there is public demand, a receptive professional leadership in the schools, and inexpensive and all but self-teaching instructional materials.

More recent studies suggest that the rate is faster than was found by Ross and Mort. In a study of the rate of adoption of a mathematics programme in a county, Carlson (1964) found that almost 50 per cent of superintendents had adopted it by the fifth year. He did, however, find the same S-shaped curve noted by Ross and Mort, representing the acceptance process over time, which indicated that the adoption rate was slow in the early period, much faster in the middle period, and then slow again. Carlson's explanation of this phenomenon is that adoption is not an independent and isolated act since adopters influence each other. Brickell (1961) agrees that the rate of innovation has increased. He noted that the rate of innovation in New York State more than doubled within fifteen months of the launching of the first Russian sputnik.

While accepting that the rate of educational innovation has speeded up, several writers feel that it is still too slow and they offer either reasons why this is so or proposals to increase the rate still further. Differing adoption rates for different innovations are noted, thus indicating that the nature of the innovation itself might be an influential factor (Carlson, 1965). In a review of a number of studies it was noted that some of the significant factors were cost of the innovation, congruence with the system and support during implementation (Miles, 1964c).

It is argued that research should be linked to innovation for a number of reasons, one being the relationship between research and the speed of innovation. One effect of research is thought to be that it might eventually increase the speed of innovation if the results are favourable to the innovator. It is also suggested that results might compare the rate of diffusion of different kinds of innovation in order to try to show what are the chief supports and resistance to innovations (Young, 1965).

Another view is that education might learn from the experience of agricultural innovation in the United States with its technological revolution and its use of change agents. Coombs (1968) puts forward the following hypothesis:

> Before the creation and adoption of innovations can be greatly speeded up, there must be, first, a widespread transformation of the attitude toward change in education – by the public and educators alike; second, the creation within education of new institutional means and personnel whose prime concern is to seek improvements and innovations; and third, the fostering within teacher training colleges of attitudes that help make future teachers more receptive to innovations, thereby enabling education to engage in a vigorous and continuing process of self-renewal and advancement. (p. 119)

The second proposal, relating to 'new institutional means and personnel', is discussed later in this book.

Several reasons are offered as a partial explanation of the slow rate of innovation in schools. The first is the absence of a change agent who is outside of and free from the school he is trying to change. Secondly, it is claimed that schools are handicapped in innovation activities by the weakness of the knowledge base of new educational practices, and it is pointed out that it is rare for an educational innovation to be backed by solid research and even rarer for one to be fully developed and subjected to rigorous trial and experimentation. The third reason concerns the organisational characteristics of schools and particularly the relationship between the school as an organisation and its clients. Reference is also made to the 'domesticated organisation' of schools which means that the organisation is protected and cared for in a number of ways. It does not compete for clients; a steady flow is normally assured. There is no struggle for survival; existence is guaranteed. Funds are not closely related to performance. As a result of this kind of security and stability the need for and interest in innovation are reduced (Carlson, 1965). (In some cases, some of these characteristics are no longer present and this raises the question of whether their absence might act as a stimulus to innovation.) The lack of incentive for schools to adopt new ways is given as a further explanation of the slow rate of innovation and a contrast is made with the profit motive in business or industry. In addition there is the difficulty of assessing the extent of the success of educational innovations which acts as a disincentive (Owens, 1970).

A wider view suggests a number of factors which inhibit the rate of innovation, some general and others more specific to education. Traditionalism, laziness, fear and insecurity are the general factors mentioned. It is acknowledged that traditionalism is not always bad since stability may be desirable in some circumstances. Fear of failure is considered to dull the appetite for innovation, especially in those who have an established professional reputation. Innovation requires hard work and it is suggested that 'too often an aura of respectable consideration is used to clothe the ulterior motive of laziness' (Miller, 1967, p. 10). Miller also suggests a number of more specific factors that might affect the rate of innovation in education: the rut of experience which can give a false security (but which can also have a positive side), administrative reticence, educational bureaucracy, insufficient finance, community indifference and resistance, inadequate pre- and in-service teacher education programmes and inadequate knowledge about the process of change. Miller, like other writers, regards this factor as the major obstacle and he makes three additional points about it, which he describes as 'myths'. He believes that it is the political scientist's concept of planned change that is imagined, rather than that of the social psychologist, and that planned change is thought of by some with overtones of *1984* and *Brave New World*. He believes, too, that there is a widespread notion that a good product will succeed on its own merits and that the introduction of new educational ideas can be final: 'Too often an innovation is introduced as "the answer" rather than as something good but not perfect that can be improved with experience and careful study' (Miller, 1967, pp. 17–18).

Some teachers may well disagree with those writers who argue that the rate of innovation is still too slow, pointing out that the past two decades have seen schools involved in considerable innovation. In response to this viewpoint, some observers would claim that few innovations are having a profound effect on pupils' learning, and so there emerges an image of much superficial innovation, perhaps justifying Musgrove's (1973) reference to 'already routine and rather tired practices' and Nisbet's (1974) 'cheap, meretricious and gimmicky' innovation.

To devote time, energy and resources to innovative efforts which have such outcomes is both wasteful and disappointing. Moreover, recognition of factors that might inhibit innovation is the first stage in overcoming the problems, and later sections of this book will be concerned with a more detailed consideration of these.

REASONS FOR AND SOURCES OF INNOVATION

While it might be thought by some that the rate of innovation in education is still too slow, it is generally accepted that the rate has accelerated in recent years. The launching of the first Soviet satellite in 1957 is often cited as marking the beginning of the upsurge of innovation in the United States which was seen as necessary if the nation was to survive. However, there are other reasons besides competition with other nations for an increase in educational innovation.

Schools as social institutions will tend to change more rapidly during periods of general social change. The growing demands of an affluent society for a more highly educated workforce and for increased cultural aesthetic activities are also related to educational innovation. Growth in knowledge in contemporary America and increases in technological ability to handle and retrieve information are considered to be influential on both the content and rate of educational innovations. The size and growth of the educational establishment itself is seen as exerting perhaps the most profoundly innovative effect of all (Miles, 1964a).

From an English viewpoint, similar reasons are offered. The growth in knowledge, population increase which has resulted in greater pressures on education, and the egalitarian influence which has resulted in the raising of minimum standards of education, have all brought about innovations (Young, 1965).

The presence of large numbers of unmotivated students is given as another reason for innovation. It is also suggested that the growth of knowledge has not only made the traditional syllabus obsolete but has led to a weakening of the boundaries of academic disciplines. Some educators innovate not only because they feel that existing arrangements are inadequate but also to relieve their own boredom. Innovation dispels, if only briefly, 'the fog of boredom that hovers over everything we do in our classrooms' (Trow, 1970, p. 291). This unusual viewpoint is taken even further by the suggestion that innovations in education can be justified for their own sake almost regardless of their outcomes.

While many writers speak with confidence about the reasons for innovation, Hoyle is less sure about the sources of innovation in education. He writes: 'We know almost nothing about the sources of new ideas in education, whether these are largely conceived in the school to be taken up or promoted by outside bodies, or whether most of the new ideas in education are generated outside the school' (1969, p. 136). Other writers, however, do not share Hoyle's uncertainty. It is recognised that it is difficult to innovate in permanent systems because they are directing most of their available energy towards carrying out routine operations and maintaining existing relationships, and it is claimed that the majority of educational innovations have their source outside the school (Miles, 1964b). This view is shared by several writers including Brickell (1964), Griffiths (1964) and Dahllöf (1970), Griffiths arguing that the degree and duration of innovation are directly proportional to the intensity of the stimulus from outside.

A number of specific sources of innovations in the United States are suggested: classroom teachers, administrators, school boards, lay public, state departments of education, education faculties in colleges and universities, professional associations, the United States Office of Education and other federal government agencies, textbook publishers and experts in mathematics and sciences are all cited as extremely significant sources (Pellegrin, 1967).

An interesting contrasting viewpoint from the United Kingdom is put forward by Owen (1973) and Hoyle (1974). Owen lists official edicts, the philosophies of educational visionaries, people, books, tradition and history, but argues that the strongest influence on curriculum innovation has been exercised by the education system. The people to whom Owen refers are members of Her Majesty's Inspectorate, local authority inspectors and advisers, headteachers and those organising in-service education. Similar possible influences are discussed by Hoyle. He makes the important point that because the British education is relatively decentralised the possibility of influence is high, while the possibility of coercion is very low. Hoyle refers to the influence of both national and local government and mentions the fact that certain local education authorities which are associated with particular forms of innovation exert influence through the allocation of resources, the selection of headteachers and other staff, the guidance given by inspectors and advisers and the kind of in-service education provided. Other sources of influence on innovation in schools mentioned by Hoyle are such agencies as the Schools Council and the external examining boards; he also refers to the significance of the growing influence of parents.

The headteacher has been mentioned as an important influence on innovation. Two research studies suggest that while the headteacher is frequently the initiator of innovation in his own school it is doubtful if he is the source of the innovative ideas. A study of fifteen innovative primary schools indicates that the headteacher was usually the impetus for innovation but that he was greatly influenced by members of Her Majesty's Inspectorate, the mass media and official publications such as the Plowden Report (Brown, 1971). In a study of the headteacher as innovator in fifteen secondary schools, twelve of the headteachers said that they had been the source of the initial idea for the innovation but in reality, in ten of the cases, the initial idea had come from elsewhere. The initial idea for the innovation came from outside in eleven out of the fifteen schools and from inside in the remaining four. While several agencies were mentioned as being responsible for the initial idea, the most influential was that of in-service courses attended by the headteachers (Dickinson, 1975).

WHAT NEEDS TO BE PLANNED AND WHY

There are several major elements associated with the implementation of an innovation. There is the innovation itself with its own particular characteristics. There are the teachers who are to be involved and affected. The teachers will have varying attitudes to innovation in general and to the particular innovation, varying strengths and weaknesses and perhaps also varying fears and doubts. The third element in the picture is the particular setting into which the innovation is to be introduced. This, too, will have particular characteristics, form of organisation and procedures. Bringing these three elements together are the processes of planning and management which it is hoped will lead to successful implementation.

All these factors with their many and varied characteristics are likely to affect the extent to which implementation of an innovation takes place. They indicate the complexities involved and also suggest the nature of the difficulty of bringing about successful innovation. Each factor, with its many variations and particular characteristics, has to be taken into account.

Planning presents a means of doing this systematically and a systematic approach is more likely to lead to successful innovation which has a significant impact on learning. It draws attention to all the factors involved and provides greater control. As was suggested earlier, systematic planning enables a considered response to be made to the demands of a rapidly changing society and may possibly provide schools with the means by which they can resist being overwhelmed by such demands. The nature of present-day innovations is seen by Hoyle (1970) as a further reason for planning when he suggests that 'the cost, complexity and radical nature of current innovations perhaps renders inappropriate the reliance upon the rather *ad hoc* and individualistic response that one has had in the past' (p. 2).

The planning and management of educational innovations is the concern of the remainder of this book. It is important at this stage to clarify the distinction and relationship between curriculum development and the planning and management of innovations. Curriculum development is an integral part of the wider process of the management of innovation. If teachers decide to create their own innovation they will be involved in considerable curriculum development activity. If it is decided to use an innovation developed outside the school there is likely to be a certain amount of curriculum development in modifying or adapting it. In both cases curriculum development is one phase in the process of innovation. Other phases leading up to the decision either to develop a school-based innovation or to bring in an externally developed one will have gone before, and others leading to its implementation will follow. Further curriculum development might take place later as a result of evaluation. This book is concerned with the management of educational innovations, which might be organisational as well as curriculum innovations. Inevitably references will be made to curriculum development in this book but this is not essentially its concern. Major issues which will be considered are the selection of innovations, their introduction and maintenance, the human factor, the role of the head or principal, the nature of the setting in which innovation takes place and the evaluation of innovations. These are issues that are of concern not only to those in schools who have responsibility for the management of innovation, whether these are headteachers, senior management teams, heads of department, or curriculum planning groups, but also to those teachers who are likely to be involved with innovation, either from choice or as a result of decisions made by others.

Chapter 2

Selecting an Innovation

Once a decision has been taken that it is either desirable or necessary to innovate, or at least that there are weaknesses or deficiencies to be remedied in the present system, among the factors which require early consideration are, first, where the particular innovation will come from, and secondly, how it will be introduced into the school. In relation to the innovation, a number of sources may be available to the innovator. There may be a nationally published project or course that could be considered; another school known to the innovator may have adopted an innovation that could be looked at; a group in a local teachers' centre may have developed an innovation in a relevant area. If these or other sources are not fruitful and nothing considered appropriate is already in existence, teachers in the school will have to develop their own innovation. On the other hand, in some instances a school-developed innovation may be the first choice. Innovations developed or disseminated in these different ways tend to have distinctive characteristics; a study of the bases on which innovations are developed, disseminated and utilised, that is, models of innovation, will help in the identification of possible strengths and weaknesses of the alternatives that are available.

MODELS OF INNOVATION

A large body of the literature on innovation consists of attempts to analyse changes that have already taken place and from these analyses, models are abstracted in order to help future planned change. One of the writers in this area is Havelock (1969, 1971); his major work (1969) reviews 4,000 studies of change in many fields including education and is aimed at policy-makers and practitioners. The models identified by Havelock and also those of Schon (1971) will be presented here.

Havelock's major conclusion is that the principal models of dissemination and utilisation of knowledge used by most people can be grouped under three perspectives: first, research, development and diffusion; secondly, social interaction; and thirdly, problem-solving. Having identified the three models, Havelock goes on to argue that the three can be synthesised in a linkage model which incorporates important features of them all.

Research, Development and Diffusion Model (RDD)
This model regards the process of change as a rational series of activities in which an innovation is discovered or invented, then developed, produced and disseminated to the user. The initiative in this model lies with the researchers, developers and disseminators while the receiver remains passive. As Havelock puts it: 'Although consumer needs may be implicit in this approach, they do not enter the picture as prime motivators for the generation of new knowledge' (ch. 2, p. 42). Research is not concerned with a set of answers to specific human problems, but rather with a set of facts and theories which generate ideas for useful products and services which are turned into prototypes that are tested and redesigned. Following this development phase, innovations are then ready to be diffused to anyone who might find them useful.

Havelock identifies the major characteristics of the RDD model as follows:

(1) It assumes a rational sequence of activities from research to development to dissemination.
(2) It implies that planning on a large scale has taken place.
(3) It involves a division of labour with a clear separation of roles and functions.
(4) It assumes a passive consumer who is willing to accept the innovation.
(5) It involves a high level of initial development costs before dissemination takes place.

While this model perhaps does not exist in a pure form in education, such projects as Nuffield Science and Nuffield Mathematics and some of the Schools Council curriculum projects come close to it. The innovator, therefore, might have available to him an innovation developed on this model which he could consider. He is likely to find that it is of a very high quality, well packaged and presented, and with professionally produced materials. Clearly, such characteristics will make a good impression, but there are other factors which the innovator should take into account. He should consider whether the aims and objectives, stated or implied, are compatible with those of the school. In general, nationally produced courses and materials tend to be more radical than those developed by teachers and there is some evidence that teachers tend to impose on them their own philosophy and pedagogy (Bealing, 1972; Hamilton, 1975; Eggleston *et al.*, 1976). The innovator needs to ask himself whether an innovation is sufficiently congruent with the philosophy, practice and ability of the teachers who are to use it. In essence, the problem is that educational innovations developed on the basis of the RDD model, however impressive their quality, may not be appropriate for all schools. Indeed, the Schools Council itself (Tomlinson, 1978) has expressed disappointment that its projects have lacked impact on work in schools.

Social Interaction Model (SI)

The main concern of this model is the way in which innovations are spread. It assumes that any research and development have already been carried out. The social interaction model emphasises diffusion, the movement of messages from person to person and from system to system. In this model an innovation is brought to the attention of a potential receiver. It is the sender who determines both the receiver and the receiver's needs. The receiver reacts to the innovation presented to him and it is the nature of his reaction which determines subsequent stages. If, having been made aware of the innovation, he shows interest in it, there follows a series of stages which culminates in acceptance or rejection of the innovation. The receiver moves through these stages by means of a process of social interaction with members of his group, and so diffusion in this model depends greatly on channels of communication. It is a model that emphasises the importance of opinion leadership, personal contact and social relationships. Characteristics of the model are:

(1) The individual user or adopter belongs to a network of social relations which largely influence his adopter behaviour.
(2) His place in the network (centrality, peripherality, isolation) is a good predictor of his rate of acceptance of new ideas.
(3) Informal personal contact is a vital part of the influence and adoption process.
(4) Group membership and reference group identifications are major predictors of individual adoption.
(5) The rate of diffusion through a social system follows a predictable S-curve pattern (very slow rate at the beginning, followed by a long late-adopter or 'laggard' period). (Havelock, 1971, p. 86).

The studies of innovation in primary and secondary schools carried out by Brown (1971) and Dickinson (1975) respectively suggest that the headteacher frequently gets his innovative ideas from what Hoyle (1974) calls the 'messengers of innovation' who include advisers, inspectors and those conducting in-service courses. Teachers, too, are in contact with these 'messengers' although usually to a lesser extent than are headteachers. Teachers and headteachers are also in personal contact with colleagues in other schools, both informally and in teachers' centres, at meetings of professional bodies, and so on, and these too may constitute a source of information about innovations. Not all the characteristics of the social interaction model are necessarily present in the diffusion of innovations in the education world, but usually several of them are in evidence.

A headteacher who wishes to innovate may find that an innovation which might suit his needs is in operation in a local school where he can go to see it in action. He may well feel that if teachers in a neighbouring school can cope effectively with it then his own teachers are likely to be able to do so. Moreover, his teachers can also see the innovation in action which might help acceptance and implementation. These factors may give the potential innovator some reassurance and the confidence to proceed. However, there might be problems associated with innovations derived from this model. One problem concerns the transferability of an innovation from one school to another: an innovation that is appropriate for one school may not be so for another, and what works in one school may not in another. Problems related to congruence, mentioned with reference to innovations developed on the RDD model, may also be present here.

Problem-Solving Model
In contrast to the other two models, the user in the problem-solving model is seen as an active participant and not as a passive receiver. In this model the need of the receiver, whether implied, stated, or assumed, is the focal point. The stages in this process of change can be viewed as a cycle, beginning with a felt need which is articulated as a problem. There follows a search for solutions, from which one is selected and applied. If the solution is an appropriate one it leads to a reduction of the original felt need. If it is not the right solution, the search is repeated until an approriate need-reducing solution is found. In this model the solution of the problem is undertaken by the receiver himself or with the help of suitable outside assistance, usually referred to as a 'change agent'. Havelock stresses that if they are to be effective, change agents should act as collaborators and not as directors.
Advocates of this orientation to innovation usually emphasise five points:

(1) User need is the paramount consideration, this being the only acceptable value-stance for the change agent; what the user needs and what the user thinks he needs are the primary concern of any would-be helper.
(2) Diagnosis of need always has to be an integral part of the total process.
(3) The outside change agent should be non-directive, rarely, if ever, violating the integrity of the user by setting himself up as the 'expert'.

(4) Internal resources, that is, those resources already existing and easily accessible within the client system itself, should always be fully utilised.

(5) Self-initiated and self-applied innovation will have the strongest user commitment and the best chances for long-term survival. (Havelock, 1971, p. 90)

Whereas innovations developed or disseminated in the RDD and social interaction models have their origins outside the particular school in which they might eventually be adopted, the problem-solving model takes us into the field of school-based innovation. In addition to the increased possibility of teacher commitment and of long-term survival just mentioned, there are other advantages associated with innovations developed through the problem-solving model. They will be, by definition, appropriate for the particular school in which they have been developed and, therefore, will be unlikely to create difficulties related to conflict of aims and pedagogy and of congruence, often associated with innovations developed outside a particular school. These are powerful advantages which, however, need to be balanced by consideration of possible weaknesses or problems associated with this model, particularly as there is considerable support at the present time for school-based innovation.

Some of these are raised by Becher and Maclure (1978) who point first to the fact that a head and his staff, described as 'temporary incumbents of a public institution', can impose their own values on a school. In some notable examples these have been at such variance with the rest of society, parents in particular, that there has been a public outcry (Berg, 1968; Auld, 1976); Gretton and Jackson, 1976). More often, however, since changes tend to be piecemeal they escape public attention. Becher and Maclure raise a more general objection which they put as follows:

There is the more general objection that school-based curriculum development reflects the limitations of sympathy, understanding and cultural bent (not to mention technical skill in course construction and preparation of classroom materials of the handful of individual teachers who happen to form the directing group at the top of the school. What if these sympathies and understandings are too narrow, or if the collective cultural orientation is unbalanced or eccentric? (1978, p. 171)

Similar issues are raised and expressed rather more strongly by Musgrove and Taylor (1969):

An educated democracy requires that the teacher shall be an expert in means rather than an arbiter of ends – which he is in fact within the broad framework of control maintained by the local authorities, whose elected members have virtually no say over the detailed provision of education, the curriculum of the schools and their extra-curricular activities. What is so remarkable is that a nation so self-righteous about its liberties should continue to tolerate at the very centre of its being the kind of creatures its children shall be, their life-style, their life-chances. Perhaps it is tolerated only because it is, in general, such a thoroughly unadventurous despotism, shaping nothing more outrageous than a standardized utility product. (p. 85)

These fundamental issues of values, limitations of understanding and the right to determine the curriculum are matters to be resolved by society at large, although those with responsibility for running schools need to be alert to the dangers and problems. A more practical problem, and one which headteachers can take steps to remedy, is that of limitation of technical skill in course construction and preparation of classroom materials mentioned by Becher and Maclure. It might be thought that this skill is part of the stock-in-trade of all teachers and yet there is some evidence to suggest that many teachers do not possess it to a high degree. This was the case in the Smith and Keith (1971) study of Kensington, the Gross *et al.* (1971) study of Cambire and the present writer's (1979) study of an English comprehensive school given the fictitious name of Heathfield. This problem and ways of resolving it are discussed more fully later.

Another problem associated with school-based innovation is that it is rarely, if ever, based on research, which the problem-solving model assumes has been carried out. The study of Heathfield (Nicholls, 1979) showed that the teachers gave no attention at all to the educational principles underlying the major dimensions of the innovation, let alone engaged in any research. Such neglect usually leads to the lack of rigour and the superficiality in innovation noted by several writers (Schmuck and Miles, 1971; Bealing, 1972; Eggleston, *et al.*, 1976) Tomlinson, 1978). One strong advocate of school-based innovation, Stenhouse (1975), has urged the adoption by teachers of a research and development role, and Elliott and Adelman (1974) have demonstrated one way of achieving this.

The description of the problem-solving model of innovation notes that the solution of the problem may be achieved with or without the use of an external change agent. The use of a change agent in schools in the United Kingdom is rare and many headteachers and teachers might find the idea quite unacceptable. An argument for using an external change agent will be presented later in the book.

These three models identified by Havelock do not exist in the education field in a 'pure' form, in the sense that all the characteristics associated with each are present. There is also a lack of purity in another sense, in that an educational innovation may be associated with more than one model. This can be seen in the case of an innovation in a neighbouring school seen by or brought to the attention of teachers in another school. While this particular innovation is diffused by means of the social interaction model it might have had its origins in either the RDD or the problem-solving model. It could be a nationally developed project being used in its intended form or, more likely, in a much modified form. The modifications might have been made for positive reasons to make it more appropriate for the particular situation, or for more negative reasons, such as teachers' inability or reluctance to cope with certain aspects of it. On the other hand, the innovation might have been developed in the neighbouring school to solve a particular problem in that school.

There are other permutations possible and this emphasises the need for the would-be innovator to scrutinise most carefully and to find out as much as possible about the origins of an innovation before trying to introduce it into his school.

Schon (1971) presents other models of innovation; he argues that the loss of the stable state means that society and its institutions are in a continuing process of change and that we must learn how to understand, guide, influence and manage these transformations. It is not enough, claims Schon, for us to be able to transform our institutions in response to changing situations; we must invent and develop institutions which are 'learning systems', that is, systems capable of bringing about their own continuing transformation.

Centre–Periphery Model
Schon's first model rests on three basic elements:

1 The innovation to be diffused exists, fully realised, in its essentials, prior to its diffusion.
2 Diffusion is the movement of an innovation from a centre out to its eventual users.
3 Directed diffusion is a centrally managed process of dissemination, training and provision of resources and inventions.

He argues that the effectiveness of this model depends on the level of resources and energy at the centre, the number of points at the periphery, the length of the radii, or spokes, through which diffusion takes place and the energy needed to gain a new adoption. According to Schon, the scope of this model 'varies directly with the level of technology governing the flows of men, materials, money and information' and depends on the system's 'capacity for generating and managing feedback' (1971, p. 82). Failure in this model takes the form of ineffectiveness in diffusion, distortion of the message, or disintegration of the whole system. Failure occurs when the system exceeds the resources or the energy at the centre, overloads the capacity of the radii, or mishandles feedback from the periphery.

Schon notes two important variants of the centre–periphery model: the 'Johnny Appleseed' and 'magnet' models. He compares the 'Johnny Appleseed' model to a kind of bard who roams about spreading a new message, whereas the 'magnet' model attracts agents of diffusion to it, as, for instance, universities have long since done. Schon sees the advantages of the 'magnet' model as tighter control of teaching and greater efficiency in the use of teachers, and the disadvantages as less control over what happens afterwards and less variation in adaptation to the particular needs of the outposts. On the other hand, the 'Johnny Appleseed' model allows for adaptation to special conditions, but offers less opportunity for 'the development of a critical mass at the centre capable of attracting new adherents' (p. 83).

It is clear that there are certain similarities between Schon's centre –periphery model and Havelock's RDD model and so some of the strengths and weaknesses already mentioned in connection with educational innovations developed in the latter would also apply to those developed in the former. However, Schon's conceptualisation throws into focus other issues which can be studied by examining the way in which many of the Schools Council's curriculum projects (which are examples of innovations developed in the centre–periphery model) operated. The project team constituted the centre and they, sometimes with the help of teachers, developed the innovation which, after trials, was disseminated to schools, the points at the periphery. The extent to which training was necessary depended on the extent to which the innovations departed from usual practice in schools. Project teams were usually based in colleges or universities and, although they travelled throughout the country providing support, those schools using the innovation located near to the project's base would be in a position to receive greater support than those more distant. Moreover, resources were not sufficient for support to be provided for every school using the innovation and eventually project teams were disbanded and support was no longer available. Distortion of the project team's message took the form of teachers imposing their own philosophy and using the innovation in ways or in a form other than the team intended. For those schools wishing to adopt the innovation in its intended form the availability of support from the project team was a considerable benefit. Once teams are disbanded a teachers' manual is the usual form of support; for many Schools Council projects this is the only form of support now available.

The 'Johnny Appleseed' variant is similar to Havelock's social interaction model. In an educational context Schon's bard is usually the inspector or adviser who spreads his innovation messages as he goes from school to school. The advantages and disadvantages of innovations developed in this model have already been mentioned. Schon also notes the problem of diffuseness associated with this model which could mean a lack of impact.

The 'magnet' model also has some of the characteristics of the social interaction model and is exemplified as in-service education for teachers. Dickinson's (1975) study indicated the importance of in-service courses as a source of innovative ideas for headteachers. The problems of adaptation to particular situations have already been discussed.

Proliferation-of-Centres Model
This is an elaboration of the centre–periphery model, designed to extend the limits of the simpler model and overcome the sources of failure that are inherent in it. It retains the basic centre–periphery structure but distinguishes between primary and secondary centres. Primary centres support secondary centres which are engaged in the diffusion of innovations, thus increasing both reach and efficiency. Each secondary centre has the scope of what would have been the whole system in the centre–periphery model. In the proliferation model the primary centre is a trainer of trainers and specialises in training, deployment, support, monitoring and management. According to Schon, when this model fails the secondary centres get out of control. Sources of failure are variants of the conditions that bring about failure in the simpler centre–periphery model. The network of communication involving money, men, information and materials may prove inadequate for the demands made on it. Demands on leadership and management may become too heavy for the system as the primary centre takes on new responsibilities. The motivation of the agent of diffusion may be threatened in the face of uncertainty of direction at the centre or when the centre seems unresponsive to local needs. Another possible source of failure is the conflict between regional diversity and rigidity of the central doctrine.

An educational innovation that was diffused through a model which was very similar to the proliferation-of-centres model is the Humanities Curriculum Project. One feature of this innovation is that the teacher acts in a non-directive manner. Because this constitutes a such radical departure from normal teaching activity, some forms of training and support were considered necessary. In some areas of the country the project team provided such training to small groups of key people in teachers' centres which, in relation to this innovation, then became secondary centres able to perform two major functions. They were in a position to offer their expertise to help those who had already made a decision to adopt the innovation, and they were also able to offer in-service courses which might, in fact, have assisted in the diffusion of the innovation. The presence of knowledgeable, experienced and helpful people in the locality would have provided the kind of encouragement and reassurance mentioned in connection with the social interaction model. In some cases, the secondary centres might also have helped to prolong the life of the innovation well beyond the existence of the project team.

Before leaving this discussion of models, reference needs to be made to the sequence of events mentioned in the opening paragraph of this chapter where it was suggested that a decision is made to innovate and then an appropriate innovation is selected or created. While this might be the most logical sequence it is not the one which always operates in schools. It is not unusual for an innovation to come to the attention of a teacher or teachers and then for a decision to be taken to adopt it. Whatever the sequence of events, a knowledge of models is helpful to the innovator. As suggested earlier, such knowledge can help the innovator to identify strengths and weaknesses inherent in each. The strengths associated with innovations developed or disseminated according to a particular model might encourage the adoption of one of these, should an appropriate innovation exist. Knowledge of the possible weaknesses or difficulties would forearm the innovator and alert him to the need to take precautionary or remedial measures.

CHARACTERISTICS OF INNOVATIONS

In addition to the way in which innovations are developed and disseminated, it is also claimed that certain characteristics are important factors in determining the extent to which they are adopted and implemented. As Barnett (1953) puts it: 'The reception given to a new idea is not so fortuitous and unpredictable as it sometimes appears to be. The character of the idea itself is an important determinant' (p. 313).

Several classifications of characteristics of innovations are presented in the literature and they have much in common (see Barnett, 1953; Rogers, 1962; Miles, 1964c; Havelock, 1969; Rogers and Shoemaker, 1971). The classification proposed by Rogers and Shoemaker will be discussed here. They identify five characteristics: relative advantage, compatibility, complexity, trialability and obser-

quote to support their generalisation is not drawn from education. This is not to say, however, that trialability is not a useful characteristic to consider. It might be helpful in many instances if teachers were to try out innovations on a small scale and carefully monitor and evaluate them before proceeding further. Once a commitment to an innovation has been made and much time, energy and effort expended in its development and implementation, there is a strong reluctance to discontinue it. Innovation undertaken in this way is unlikely to lead to the creation of a self-renewing school, but rather to the replacement of one fixed and rigid practice by another.

Observability

Rogers and Shoemaker define this as 'the degree to which the results of an innovation are visible to others' (1971, p. 155). They point out that the results of some ideas are easily observed and communicated to others, while some innovations are difficult to describe. They believe that observability is positively related to the adoption of an innovation. There is some support from the field of education for this view in the studies of innovating schools carried out by Dickinson (1975). He found in the schools he studied that there was an acceptance of innovation that could be seen to be working successfully in other schools and that it was innovation of this kind to which the schools studied were most susceptible.

It would appear that this evidence presents the manager of innovation with a dilemma. On the one hand there is some evidence to suggest that if he introduces an innovation into his school which can be seen in a neighbouring school, it is likely to be accepted and implemented. On the other hand it has already been noted that what is appropriate in one school does not necessarily match the needs of another. In introducing an innovation which is in use elsewhere, especially if it is done without a careful analysis and evaluation, an innovator may be open to the criticism of jumping on the innovation bandwagon, and could find himself on the innovation hearse (Nisbet, 1974).

The idea underlying the identification of characteristics of innovations by various writers is to relate the characteristics to the rate of adoption of innovations. The writers are concerned to try to account for the fact that some innovations seem to be more acceptable than others. It has to be acknowledged that there is not a large body of empirical research to demonstrate the effects of characteristics of innovations on adoption. The five characteristics identified by Rogers and Shoemaker (1971), which constitute the most recent of several classifications, are based on 'past writings and research as well as on a desire for maximum generality and succinctness' (p. 137). There is, as well as some research evidence and observations based on experience, a 'common-sense' aspect to the characteristics. Careful thought by experienced teachers about the characteristics of relative advantage, compatibility and complexity would suggest the probable relationship with the acceptability of innovations. The characteristics of trialability and observability are more problematic in the field of education. However, in spite of the common-sense aspect, they are factors which are frequently overlooked by innovators. They have been included here, as has an analysis of models of innovation, to draw attention to the need for managers of innovation to study in detail many aspects of innovations before they introduce them into schools.

A very important point, raised in relation to characteristics of innovations, is that it is the potential users' perceptions which are significant, rather than attributes identified by others. The implication of this point for managers of innovations is that they need to know what the perceptions of potential users are and this means that there must be full and open discussions about innovation. The issues of communication and teacher involvement are discussed fully in a later chapter.

Chapter 3

Introducing and Maintaining Innovations

Once it has been decided that an innovation is to be tried in a school, other early decisions which need to be taken concern the way in which the innovation (or the idea of the innovation) is to be introduced to the teachers who are to be involved with it and the way in which the innovation is to be developed and sustained. These decisions are likely to have profound effects on the extent to which the innovation is successfully implemented. A study of strategies will suggest the major approaches that might be taken. The term strategy is borrowed from the military field where it means the science and art of planning and directing operations against an enemy. A strategy for innovation, therefore, implies a planned and systematic attack on a problem, or as Miles (1964c) puts it, 'a general set of policies underlying specific action steps ("tactics") expected to be useful in achieving the durable installation of an innovation' (p. 648).

STRATEGIES FOR INNOVATION

A number of strategies for innovation have been identified and there is a high degree of agreement among them. One common element in all the strategies is the conscious utilisation and application of knowledge, whether of things or of people, the latter being used to help to understand the behaviour of individuals and groups. Frequently, the adoption of an educational innovation involves both, since even a specific 'thing-oriented' innovation affects the behaviour of those involved. One of the most comprehensive analyses of strategies for innovation is that offered by Chin and Benne (1976) who identify three major groups of strategies: first, empirical-rational; secondly, normative-re-educative; and thirdly, power-coercive.

Empirical-Rational Strategies
Underlying the empirical-rational group of strategies is the assumption that man is rational and that he will follow his rational self-interest once this is revealed to him. An innovation is usually suggested by someone who knows both its possible effects and the individual, group, or organisation that will be affected by the innovation.

The main task of the innovator is to show as effectively as he can the validity of the innovation in terms of the gains to be achieved by adopting it. This attitude to innovation is based on an optimistic view of man and sees the main obstacles to innovation or progress as ignorance and superstition. It advocates education as a way of disseminating scientific knowledge and of freeing man from the 'shackles of superstition'.

From the viewpoint of the innovator the empirical-rational strategies are probably the easiest to use and involve him in the least effort. He is likely to consider his colleagues to be rational human beings; he is convinced of the benefits of the proposed innovation and believes that if he communicates these to his colleagues they, too, will be convinced and therefore willing to adopt the innovation. It is, however, a deceptively simple approach, especially in relation to innovations which require people to change their behaviour. Some studies of innovation in schools have shown that the actual use of an empirical-rational approach had certain deficiencies and did not lead to a succesful implementation of innovation (Gross *et al.*, 1971; Nicholls, 1979).

Chin and Benne include a number of specific strategies within the empirical-rational approach to effecting change. These are basic research and dissemination of knowledge through general education, personnel selection and replacement, systems analysts as staff consultants, applied research and linkage systems for diffusion of research results and utopian thinking as a strategy for change. While each of these can be seen at the theoretical level to have possibilities, each also appears to have problems in relation to innovation in schools.

Normative-Re-educative Strategies

Chin and Benne's second group of strategies is based on different assumptions about human motivation from those underlying the empirical-rational. They put it as follows:

> The rationality and intelligence of men are not denied. Patterns of action and practice are supported by socio-cultural norms and by commitments on the part of individuals to these norms. Socio-cultural norms are supported by the attitude and value systems of individuals – normative outlooks which undergird their commitments. Change in a pattern of practice or action, according to this view, will occur only as the persons involved are brought to change their normative orientations to old patterns and develop commitments to new ones. And changes in normative orientations involve changes in attitudes, values, skills and significant relationships, not just changes in knowledge, information or intellectual rationales for action and practice. (p. 23)

This group of strategies has developed from theories based on the work of Dewey, Freud and Lewin; they have the following characteristics:

(1) Emphasis is on the client system and his (or its) involvement in working out programmes of change and improvement for himself (or itself).

(2) It is not assumed that the client's problem is necessarily one which may be solved by more adequate technical information. It is recognised that the problem may lie in the attitudes, values, norms and internal and external relationships of the client system and that alteration or re-education of these may be necessary to solve the problem.

(3) A change agent works collaboratively with the client in an attempt to solve the client's problem(s).

(4) Non-conscious elements which impede the solution of problems are brought into the open and examined.

(5) The change agent and client use methods and concepts drawn from the behavioural sciences to deal with problems.

One aspect of this approach to change which might be unacceptable to British schools is the use of an external change agent, a matter mentioned earlier in relation to the problem-solving model of innovation. Two brief points only will be made here in this connection. The first is to suggest that the recent support by the Department of Education and Science (DES, 1978) for school-based in-service education and the use of external consultants might help to make the idea of using a change agent more acceptable. The second point is to argue that it might be more helpful to consider the underlying assumptions of the normative-re-educative approach rather than each particular characteristic and to suggest that the spirit of the approach is more important than the details.

Chin and Benne discuss two groups of approaches within the normative-re-educative perspective. First, there is the improvement of the problem-solving capability of a system in which the emphasis is on the potentiality of the system to develop and institutionalise its own problem-solving structures and processes, which must deal both with human problems of relationship and morale and with technical problems of meeting the system's task requirements as set by its goals. The second group concerns the releasing and fostering of growth in the persons who make up the system to be changed, in which the emphasis is on the person as the basic unit of social organisation. Inherent in this approach is the assumption that people are capable of creative responses, choices and actions if conditions are appropriate.

Although Chin and Benne present the two normative-re-educative approaches in a way which emphasises their differences, they point out that there are many similarities between them. Both emphasise experience-based learning as a feature of all lasting changes in human systems and both accept the principle that people must learn to learn from their experiences if self-directed change is to be maintained and continued. Learning to learn from ongoing experience is an important objective of both approaches. Exponents of both are committed to re-education as an essential feature of effective change in human systems, and both stress norms of openness of communication, trust between persons, lowering of status barriers between parts of the system and mutuality between parts as necessary conditions of the process of re-education.

It will be obvious that these strategies for innovation present the would-be innovator with a much more difficult, complex and time-consuming task than the empirical-rational strategies previously discussed. This might be one reason why documented accounts of innovations in schools indicate that normative-re-educative strategies tend not to be used. These accounts show, among other things, that attention was focused on the specific innovation and not on the procedures and processes associated with innovating from which the participants could have derived valuable insights for further innovation (see, for example, Brown, 1971; Gross *et al.*, 1971; Smith and Keith, 1971; Dickinson, 1975; Nicholls, 1979).

Power-Coercive Strategies
Of this third group of approaches to effecting change, Chin and Benne write:

> It is not the use of power in the sense of influence by one person upon another or by one group upon another which distinguishes this family of strategies from those already discussed. Power is an ingredient of all human action. The differences lie rather in ingredients of power upon which the strategies of changing depend and the ways in which power is generated and applied in processes of affecting change. (1976, p. 39)

In the empirical–rational approaches it is knowledge which is seen as a major ingredient of power, with men of knowledge regarded as legitimate sources of power, and a desirable flow of influence or power is seen as passing from those who know to those who do not through processes of education and of dissemination of knowledge. Normative-re-educative strategies do not deny the importance of knowledge as a source of power, particularly in the form of knowledge-based technology, and advocates of this approach wish to see much greater emphasis on the use of behavioural knowledge. These strategies emphasise collaborative relationships and are opposed to coercive and non-reciprocal influence on moral and pragmatic grounds.

Power-coercive strategies emphasise political and economic sanctions and the use of moral power, playing on feelings of guilt and shame:

> In general, power-coercive strategies of changing seek to mass political and economic power behind the change goals which the strategists of change have decided are desirable. Those who oppose these goals, if they adopt the same strategy, seek to mass political and economic power in opposition. The strategy thus tends to divide the society when there is anything like a division of opinion and of power in that society. (Chin and Benne, 1976, p. 40)

Chin and Benne believe that these strategies are more widespread than most people would be willing to admit and that those out of power are not always aware that such strategies are being employed. At school level there is some evidence to suggest that power-coercive strategies are widely employed in spite of the current debate (and practice in some schools) about staff involvement in decision-making (Brown, 1971; Dickinson, 1975; Nicholls, 1979).

Three variations of power-coercive strategies are discussed by Chin and Benne. First, there are strategies of non-violence such as those used in schools, colleges and universities to highlight conflicts in values and injustices in patterns of social control. Then there is the use of political institutions to achieve change, as, for instance, in the passing of laws. Thirdly, there is the recomposition and manipulation of power élites to bring about change, a proposal put forward by Marx as a means of effecting fundamental social change. It is interesting to note that the use of re-educative strategies is seen as an essential combination of the second and third alternatives.

This leads to a consideration of the point that while these strategies have been treated separately for purposes of discussion, in practice more than one approach is likely to be used. An innovator might initially use a power-coercive strategy and follow this with a normative-re-educative strategy. More likely, however, in the school situation, would be a combination of power-coercive and empirical-rational strategies. The choice of a strategy or strategies by an innovator will depend not only on the merits of the strategies themselves but also on the nature of the innovation, the teachers who are to be involved with it and the school into which it is to be introduced.

Some of the strengths and weaknesses of the practical applications of the strategies are worthy of consideration. The empirical-rational strategies have the appeal of simplicity and ease of use. Teachers are intelligent and rational human beings and the innovator finds it reasonable to assume that if he indicates to them the advantages and merits of his innovation they will be willing to accept and implement it. Teachers, however, like other human beings, are not always rational and at times characteristics other than rationality determine their behaviour. The fact that many educational innovations exist which can be shown to offer certain advantages but which are not taken up by teachers suggests that empirical-rational strategies are not appropriate in all cases.

The advocates of normative-re-educative strategies argue that lasting and self-sustained innovation can be achieved through their use. There is some evidence to support these claims, particularly when outside consultants are used (see, for example, Schmuck and Miles, 1971). Since many educational innovations are complex and require changed attitudes, new roles and relationships, and joint planning, these strategies would seem to be the most likely to be successful as well as being most in keeping with the style of management currently advocated. However, they are both time-consuming and difficult and require knowledge and skills that might not be present in all schools and so might initially necessitate some form of external support.

Power-coercive strategies, like the empirical-rational have the attraction of simplicity and ease of use in those cases where the innovation is supported or proposed by the headteacher. He has the authority to introduce innovations into his school if he so wishes. While these strategies do not fall within what is now considered to be an appropriate style of school management they are used in some schools with some success. Probably the greatest problem associated with the use of these strategies is that of lack of real commitment or even opposition by teachers to the innovation. Notable examples of this were quoted in the Barker Lunn (1970) study of streaming. Cases were described in which headteachers had introduced the necessary administrative procedures for non-streaming but teachers continued to stream inside their classrooms.

INNOVATION AS A PROCESS

Inherent in two of the strategies, the power-coercive and the empirical-rational, is the implication that they are used by the innovator at the outset, either to force or convince acceptance of the innovation, whereas the normative-re-educative implies a longer-term activity. This is a significant difference. Accounts of innovations which were not successfully implemented point to the dangers of the innovator merely introducing the innovation to the teachers who are to be involved and leaving them to implement it. Such innovators appear to regard innovation as a single act rather than as a process, and appear to be concerned with merely introducing innovation and not with the more difficult tasks of development and maintenance. Many writers discuss and describe stages or phases in the planning, development and implementation of innovations. Carlson (1965), for example, sees an innovation as having a life-cycle:

> An educational innovation has a natural history and, in a sense, a life cycle. The full account of the life cycle of an innovation is the story of its invention, development and promotion, adoption, diffusion and demise, along with an account of the problems encountered and solutions developed in introducing and maintaining the innovation in specific settings, and the unanticipated consequences growing out of its use. (p. 4)

Not only does Carlson highlight those aspects of the life of an innovation to which the innovator needs to give attention if the attempt to innovate is to be successful, but he also indicates a means by which those involved with the innovation would learn from the experience and so become more competent in future innovating activities.

Two other views of innovation as a process will be discussed briefly. The first is that of Rogers and Shoemaker (1971) which is a modification of an earlier five-stage proposal which consisted of awareness, interest, evaluation, trial and adoption by Rogers (1962). The modified version has four stages:

(1) *Knowledge* The individual is exposed to the innovation's existence and gains some understanding of how it functions.
(2) *Persuasion* The individual forms a favourable or unfavourable attitude towards the innovation.
(3) *Decision* The individual engages in activities which lead to a choice to adopt or reject the innovation.
(4) *Confirmation* The individual seeks reinforcement for the innovation-decision he has made, but he may reverse his previous decision if exposed to conflicting messages about the innovation. (p. 103)

These stages in the innovation-decision process are seen by Rogers and Shoemaker as being one of three divisions in a wider conceptualisation of change processes, the other two being antecedents and consequences. Antecedents are those variables which are present in the situation before the innovation is introduced and consequences are those which arise from the introduction of the innovation. This conceptualisation has much in common with Carlson's life-cycle view of innovation and again draws attention to the many facets of innovation, as well as emphasising the period of time the process of innovation is likely to take.

Neither of these conceptualisations gives overt attention to evaluation (other than in making a judgement about whether or not to adopt the innovation) and both seem to be more applicable to innovations developed outside the school. There is, however, another conceptualisation of stages which includes evaluation and revision, and which is applicable to innovations that are developed both inside and outside the school. This breaks down the process of innovation into the following seven steps: problem identification and definition; innovation planning; innovation programming and development; experimentation; evaluation and revision; dissemination and revision; implementation (CERI, 1973).

There is scepticism about the usefulness of some of the conceptualisations of change as a process. Gross and his colleagues (1971), for instance, do not accept the five-stage approach to the adoption process proposed by Rogers and others as being appropriate for studying innovations in schools and other types of organisations. They argue that its lack of utility is due to certain of its assumptions which are not applicable to the implementation of organisational innovations. One basic assumption is that during any of the intermediate stages between initial awareness and ultimate use the individual is free to decide whether or not he will try the innovation, and if he tries it, whether or not he should continue with it. If he is not interested in the innovation he is free to reject it. If he does not rate it highly when he tries it he can discontinue his use of it. Gross *et al.* point out that this assumption does not apply in the case of major innovations in schools which are usually initiated by those in authority both inside and outside the school. They also suggest that the Rogers model is more applicable to the adoption of simple technological innovations by individuals and it assumes that individuals can try out innovations on a small scale without the help or support of other people. It also assumes that trials can be undertaken in an either/or fashion and that short trials provide a sufficient evaluation. As Gross *et al.* point out, many educational innovations cannot be tried out on a small scale and cannot be implemented without the co-operation and support of a number of teachers. Moreover, many educational innovations are so complex that they cannot be tried out in an either/or fashion and some may even require several years of full implementation before an adequate evaluation of their effectiveness can be given.

These criticisms are valid, but particularly important are those concerned with the pressures on teachers from those in authority to accept and continue to use innovations and the problems associated with trials (MacDonald and Ruddock, 1971; Shipman, 1974).

Nevertheless, the idea of considering the adoption, planning and implementation of an innovation as a series of stages rather than as a single event might be helpful to teachers. There are many examples in the literature of conceptualisations of innovation as a process on which teachers might draw, either to use as they exist or to modify to suit their own circumstances. Several writers have shown that teachers involved in innovation are usually expected to carry out all the related activities themselves with little or no support (Gross *et al.*, 1971; Smith and Keith, 1971; CERI, 1973; Hoyle, 1974; Nicholls, 1979). A recognition of the existence of stages and of the activities associated with each stage in the process of innovation might encourage the innovator to realise the magnitude of the task, to carry out monitoring over a period of time and to provide support of various kinds for the teachers involved when and where necessary.

ACTIVITIES RELATED TO STAGES

If the process of innovation is broken down into stages, the innovator has to consider what activities are related to each stage and who is best able to undertake them. The nature of these activities will depend on both the innovator's conceptualisation of the process of innovation and circumstances into which it is to be introduced, but it might be helpful to examine the way in which some writers see these activities.

Rubin (1968, p. 159), for example, states that 'the effective installation of an innovation in a school requires three sequential operations, each involving a number of discrete steps: preliminary analysis, strategy selection and action'. (It should be noted that Rubin is not using the term strategy in the same sense as it was used earlier in this chapter.) He elaborates on these three operations as follows:

I   Preliminary analysis:
   1   diagnosis of a weakness;
   2   analysis of the responsible factors;
   3   comparison of alternative correctives;
   4   selection of the best corrective.
II   Strategy selection:
   1   what kind of an innovation is to be installed?
   2   who will engineer the installation?
   3   what conditions characterise the target environment?
III   Action:
   1   analysis of the innovation's requirements in training, materials and linkage to existing systems;
   2   initiation of motivating pressures through inducing dissatisfaction and illuminating the rewards;

3 initiation of the influencing strategy;
4 initiation of the preparatory activities;
5 installing the innovation;
6 supporting the transition from old to new;
7 linking the innovation to the permanent system. (pp. 160–1)

Rubin makes an important point concerning innovative activities when he emphasises that no action should be taken 'until a specific weakness has been identified, the target environment has been analysed, various solutions to overcoming the weakness have been considered and a rational selection of an innovation has occurred' (p. 162).

A somewhat different approach is taken by Trump (1967), who bases his procedures for initiating innovation on his 'personal experiences in working with secondary schools for more than three decades' (p. 66). He outlines and then describes five steps to be taken:

(1) Analyse co-operatively reasons for present practices.
(2) Discover what people want that is different from what they are doing.
(3) Make tentative decisions about the priority of proposed changes.
(4) Plan the innovation carefully in terms of teacher preparation, student preparation, procedures to be followed and the anticipated effects of the innovation.
(5) Determine the times and techniques for evaluation.

Watson (1967) takes a completely different perspective on the steps to be taken in what he describes as continuous self-renewal. He proposes ten steps derived from analyses of the process of constructive thinking and problem-solving. The steps are: sensing, screening, diagnosing, inventing, weighing, deciding, introducing, operating, evaluating and revising; and he says: 'Success at each step is partly a matter of cognitive clarity about the goal and appropriate methods of each process. Success depends also on emotional involvement, on skills which need to be developed, and on social structures which will encourage and sustain the desired attitudes' (p. 110).

These examples serve to illustrate that, although there are some elements in common, there are differences in the way writers see the activities related to stages in the process of innovation. They are indications of personal opinions, albeit based on wide experience, and tend to be vague. It is not difficult to identify weaknesses and omissions in the proposals. However, they do emphasise the complexity of the activities associated with innovation and draw attention to the fact that one set of people may not possess the knowledge and skills needed to undertake these activities, so that different tasks may have to be carried out by different people.

In showing that there is no general agreement about the steps involved in innovation, the examples might encourage innovators to propose their own steps. Like so many other facets of innovating, a proposal of this kind worked out for a particular school in relation to a particular innovation may be the most appropriate. This is not to suggest that the ideas and proposals of others should be disregarded, but rather that they should be considered and perhaps used as a basis for development. The complexity of the innovation and the experience of the teachers in innovating are two factors which will influence the number of steps required.

Chapter 4

The Human Factor in Innovation

The importance of the headteacher as the initiator of innovation has already been mentioned briefly. The evidence suggests that it is usually the headteacher who takes the initiative in introducing innovations into the school, and even where this is not the case his support is necessary for any innovation proposed by a member of staff. It follows from this that the headteacher has the task of imparting his ideas for the innovation to the teachers who will be concerned, and of securing their participation. In turn, the teachers will react in some way to the proposed innovation; their reactions are an important factor in the extent to which the innovation is successfully implemented and must be taken into consideration by those proposing innovation.

INNOVATORS AND RESISTERS

Some people espouse innovations eagerly, quickly and with enthusiasm, while others are more cautious, reluctant and hesitant and may, under some circumstances, totally reject them. Discussions of these two categories of persons, usually described as innovators or resisters, feature prominently in the literature on innovation. Rogers (1962) lists the terms used in previous research to describe innovators and includes the following: advance scouts, lighthouses, pioneers, progressists, experimentals and cultural avant-garde; while Miles (1964c) adds the following: agitator, dreamer, skilful navigator, committed nut, monomaniac, fanatic and true believer, Nisbet (1974) describes the innovator as having the image of being up-to-date, efficient, responsive, professional and 'superior to the mass of common conventional people' (p. 2). Rogers (1962) points out that the innovator is not always the most respected member of his social system and that he prefers 'venturesomeness' to the respect of his peers. He plays an important role in the process of change since his adoption of an innovation causes his peers to become aware of it, and if it proves to be successful, early scepticism may turn into a recognition of its utility.

In a later work Rogers (1965), drawing on research in industrial engineering, rural sociology, anthropology and education, gives a description of the salient characteristics of innovators:

Innovators are venturesome individuals; they desire the hazardous, the rash, the avant-garde and the risky. Since no other model of the innovation exists in the social system, they must also have the ability to understand and use complex technical information. An occasional debacle when one of the new ideas adopted proves to be unsuccessful does not disquiet innovators. However, in order to absorb the loss of an unprofitable innovation, they must generally have control of substantial financial resources. (p. 57)

Miles (1964c), summing up the limited research in the field of education, points to the importance of power as a feature of innovators. Referring to their personal characteristics, he mentions strength and benevolence; intelligence and verbal ability; individualism and creativity; authenticity and enthusiasm. However, he also refers to the less heroic characteristics of innovators and suggests that they might be 'rebellious, alienated, excessively idealistic (and thus unable to cope with problems of the survival of the innovating unit), emotionally unstable and prone to resentment and rebellion in the face of adversity or disillusionment' (p. 642).

Resistance to change is seen by many writers as a frequent and strong phenomenon among members of an organisation. Overcoming this resistance is considered to be a major task in the process of change, with resisters often cast in the role of villains. Barnes (1967) refers to the folklore of change which thrives on 'accounts of courageous individuals who unilaterally defied a complacent majority' and the development of a David and Goliath syndrome: 'David, the courageous advocate of righteousness, progress, and a change of social order must slay the giants of resistance and tradition . . . Individualistic courage is praised while conformity and resistance to change are eternally condemned' (pp. 63–4). Barnes, however, presents a different viewpoint. He argues that in a process of change which includes initiation advocacy and resistance, either group (the advocates or the resisters) may, with hindsight, turn out to have been rational and reasonable while the other was not. He describes a typology in which either advocacy of or resistance to change may be accompanied by either rational or emotional behaviour. The typology consists of, first, rational advocates who propose innovations on the basis of reasoned argument; secondly, rational resisters who resist innovations on the basis of reasoned argument; thirdly, radicals who want change for the sake of change; and lastly, traditionalists who resist for the sake of resistance. Very few writers see the positive aspects of resistance. Klein is one who, like Barnes, points out that the resister may be logical and have sound reasons for his resistance, and also indicates that resisters (whom he describes as defenders) may have a role to play in the improvement of an innovation: 'In certain situations the participation of defenders in the change process may even lead to the development of more adequate plans and to the avoidance of some hitherto unforseen consequences of the projected change' (Klein, 1967, p. 33).

If the positive side of resistance is considered, the idea of over-coming resistance is no longer appropriate. It becomes more appropriate to think in terms of taking account of resistance. In other words, it may be more helpful to the successful implementation of an innovation if its advocates and supporters are prepared to listen to and consider seriously the comments of resisters.

Many other reasons for resistance to innovation are suggested in the literature. Writing specifically of teachers, Owen (1973) says that resistance is not a simple phenomenon and he describes it as arising from a mixture of misunderstanding and ignorance. Other reasons he suggests include fear, the heavy burden of work associated with innovation and the desire of some teachers, from time to time, to take the easy way out. Lippitt and his colleagues (1958) see resisters as being afraid or ignorant, as feeling inadequate, or as clinging to existing satisfactions, while Guskin (1969), drawing on research, suggests the following reasons for resistance: (1) a sense of competence and self-esteem; (2) feelings of threat and fear; (3) authoritarianism and dogmatism; and (4) a belief in self-fulfilling prophecies.

If the reasons for resistance can be so varied, advocates of an innovation face a difficult task. First, the resistance has to be identified. This is not always as simple as it might sound. In many schools it would take a great deal of courage to speak out against an innovation that is being vigorously proposed and supported by those in authority. This would be particularly true if the reasons for resistance were, for example, fear or feelings of inadequacy. So, resistance may be present but not openly expressed (Nicholls, 1979). There is also the problem of when the resistance is felt. Lippitt *et al.* (1958) note that it may emerge at the beginning of a change process or after it is under way, or both, and the Gross *et al.* (1971) study of Cambire shows how resistance developed through deficiencies in the support provided by those in authority. When any resistance has been recognised there is the task of ascertaining the causes and trying to do something about them if the innovation is not be jeopardised. Establishing causes may prove to be extremely difficult, because in some cases teachers may well feel that it is not in their best interests to admit to feelings of inadequacy or insecurity and so the reasons given may not always be the real ones. Even where it is possible to establish the genuine reasons for resistance, remedial measures may be difficult and time-consuming. However, several studies have shown that unless attention is given to the underlying causes of resistance the innovation is unlikely to be successfully implemented. Argyris

(1967), commenting on the widespread nature of resistance, notes the length of time it persists. Writing about thirty-two changes in large organisations in which he played a research and consultancy role, he makes the observation that 'after three years there were still many people fighting, ignoring, questioning, resisting, blaming the re-organization without feeling a strong obligation personally to correct the situation' (p. 53).

The frequent use in the literature of the expression 'overcoming resistance' is perhaps an unfortunate one. It gives the impression that resistance is always negative and has to be eliminated. The positive aspects of resistance have already been mentioned, but enthusiastic and committed advocates of innovation are unlikely to take account of these. This was the case in my own study of an innovation in a comprehensive school where the criticisms of the innovation by one teacher were, in my opinion, well founded, but were totally ignored by the supporters of the innovation. A consideration of the criticisms might well have led to improvements in the innovation. This led me to suggest that one of the conditions which is likely to lead to the successful implementation of innovations is that account should be taken of resistance where and when it exists (Nicholls, 1979).

PARTICIPATION IN DECISION-MAKING

Participation in decision-making is regarded by many writers as a means of coping with resistance to innovation (Argyle, 1967; Coch and French, 1948; Johns, 1973). This viewpoint stems from the concept of 'power equalization' proposed by Leavitt (1965) from which it is argued that members of an organisation will show resistance to an innovation unless they have been involved in its formulation. In order to overcome this resistance, management must share power with those who are to implement the innovation by allowing them to participate in decisions about it. Leavitt writes: 'Power equalization has thus become a key concept in several of the prevalent people theories, a first step in the causal chain leading toward organizational change' (p. 1159).

Pellegrin (1967) argues that the resister sees himself as being acted upon rather than as a participant in change and that, because of this, although he may go through the motions of change he is unlikely to internalise any alterations in his behaviour. Wilson (1966) puts forward the hypothesis that the extent to which participative management will stimulate the production of proposals or facilitate the adoption or implementation of innovations will depend, among other things, on the extent to which the decision-making group itself becomes a highly valued source of incentives and the extent to which these group-based incentives are congruent with those offered by the larger organisation.

Strauss (1963) makes a similar point in explaining the differences between the results of an American study of worker participation and a similar experiment carried out in Norway. He argues that the opportunity to participate was valued highly by the low-status rural female workers in the former study so that innovative procedures were accepted and production increased, whereas there was no increase in production in the Norwegian study because participation was less valued by the more sophisticated urban male workers. French and his colleagues (1960) offer additional explanations for the differences between the American study and their own, including the possibility that if the Norwegian workers had a stronger tradition of being organised in a union than the American workers, they might have considered participation through union representatives to be more legitimate than direct participation. The American study is also criticised on the grounds of defective design (Gardner, 1977), but it is suggested too that even if the design faults had been avoided there are factors other than participation which might have contributed to the results. These include group size, the dramatic presentation to the experimental groups, competition between two of the experimental groups, quality of training and knowledge of results given to the experimental groups.

In summarising what is known about participation, Bennis (1963) concludes that it is not clear how likely or under what circumstances participation in decision-making will improve worker satisfaction, increase productivity, or stimulate organisational innovation. Writing a little later, however, Havelock (1969) maintains that participant involvement 'may be accepted as a general "Law of Innovation" ' (ch. 10, p. 83).

Specifically in the field of education the picture is equally unclear. At the level of belief there are conflicting views. Maclure (1973) in a report of an international conference offers this observation:

> The English view ... would probably be that the case for teachers' autonomy is most formidable, not on grounds of philosophy, which is not a strong point in English education circles, but on grounds of practice – that is to say, that the best way to enlist a teacher's commitment to any innovation or to the idea of innovation as a recurrent phenomenon in education, is to implicate him in the process; because unless he is so implicated, he can and will resist and in all probability defeat the efforts of the innovators. (pp. 41–2)

However, a minority view expressed at the same conference was that teachers ought to be restricted in the kind of curriculum decisions that they could make, while one member felt that 'teachers ought *not* to have a say in the making of choices since all they knew was teaching and could not be responsible to society' (Maclure, 1973, p. 41).

From the viewpoint of teachers themselves, there would appear to be differences in the extent to which they wish to be involved in decision-making. In an American study Belasco and Alutto (1975) found that some teachers participate in more decisions than they want to (in which case they are described as decisionally-saturated), some in about the desired number, and some in fewer decisions than they would wish to (in which case they are described as decisionally-deprived). The decisionally-deprived tended to be younger males in rural secondary schools, while the decisionally-saturated, who expressed the greatest job satisfaction, tended to be older females in urban elementary schools. Belasco and Alutto suggest, like Jackson (1968) and Lortie (1969), that many teachers, particularly of younger pupils, derive their greatest satisfaction from work in the classroom with their pupils, rather than from participation in the wider affairs of the school. Hoyle (1974) has identified two categories of teachers: extended professionals and restricted professionals. One of the differences he sees between them is the extent of their desire to be involved in decision-making about school matters.

The CERI (1973) report of case studies of innovation includes the comment that while many studies of innovation start with the assumption that greater involvement of teachers in innovations automatically produces better results and faster dissemination, there is no evidence in the case studies to support this assumption. A further observation is that the Schools Council in particular, where teacher involvement is substantial, 'tends to concentrate on relatively traditional curriculum changes' (p. 188).

Gross *et al.* (1971) are critical both of the assumption that initial resistance to change is widespread and strong and of the related consequence of this assumption, that the success or failure of planned organisational change is related to the problem of overcoming resistance through participation. They comment that there is very little research evidence to support these assumptions.

Whether or not resistance to innovation is a widespread phenomenon in education and whether it manifests itself initially or at later stages of the innovation process is perhaps a matter of little significance to the advocate of an innovation who meets it at some stage in his particular school and who is concerned to do something about it. Moreover, it would be extremely naive to expect no resistance to proposed innovations. It has to be conceded that the evidence about the effects of participation is far from clear and the problem is compounded by the fact that it appears that teachers differ in the extent to which they want to be involved in decision-making.

However, despite the lack of clear evidence about the effects of participation, it is suggested here that teacher involvement in decision-making about innovation is more likely to lead to successful implementation under certain conditions and for a variety of reasons. The first reason relates to the nature of contemporary society. We live in a period in which citizens are demanding and acquiring a greater say in the way society operates. This is reflected in schools and there is certainly a great deal of discussion about a greater involvement of teachers in deciding the affairs of the school. It is difficult to establish how widespread is the actual participation of teachers and practices vary widely from school to school. Nevertheless, the climate for participation is present. Teachers are now better prepared than previously, through both initial and in-service training, for involvement in decisions about innovation and so, for this reason too, might expect and demand it.

In the earlier discussion of strategies for innovation the possible advantages of the normative-re-educative strategy in relation to lasting and self-sustained innovation were suggested. This strategy emphasises collaborative relationships and the lowering of status barriers.

An important factor that needs to be considered is the nature of participation. It has been shown previously that the most common situation is for an innovation to be proposed by the headteacher. Any discussions involving teachers are likely to be concerning details about the proposed innovation rather than about whether or not the innovation is an appropriate one for the school. Dickinson's (1975) study of innovation in secondary schools led him to the observation that there was a dearth of what he described as 'meaningful consultation' and that where there was consultation it was always about the method of implementation and administrative arrangements related to the innovation and never on its justification and relevance. This was also a feature noted in other studies of innovation (Gross *et al.*, 1971; Smith and Keith, 1971; Nicholls, 1979). It may be that participation of this kind is not highly valued by teachers and that their awareness of not having been party to the most significant decision may, at least in part, account for a lack of relationship between 'participation' and successful implementation.

Other difficulties may arise because of what might be termed 'pseudo-consultation' or 'pseudo-participation'. Teachers have quoted me examples of situations existing in their schools in which teacher committees have been set up only to have their recommendations or suggestions totally ignored or rejected. The teachers involved have had the expectation that their advice would be taken, but it was not. These situations may have arisen because of a lack of clarity about the terms of reference of the committees rather than because of a deliberate attempt to create an impression of consultation, but, whatever their cause, they can lead to feelings of frustration and ill-will and are unlikely to result in enthusiasm for the headteacher's own proposals. (Matters concerning the nature and extent of teacher participation in decision-making impinge very closely on the role of the headteacher and his style of leadership; these are discussed in the next chapter.)

The other problem mentioned earlier in connection with teacher involvement was that of teachers' own wishes for it. It is likely that in most schools, whatever their size, there will be teachers who would very much like to be involved in making decisions about innovations and their development, and others who would prefer to leave the whole matter to the headteacher and their colleagues, while they get on with the job of teaching their pupils. What is to be done about this latter group of teachers in those schools where there is provision for staff involvement? Are they to be forced to participate, perhaps making little contribution, or are they to be allowed not to, perhaps thereby being regarded by their colleagues as not accepting their full professional responsibilities? There is no clear-cut answer to this difficult problem. In a school that has participative decision-making and a climate in which such matters can be discussed constructively, this could well be an appropriate problem for the staff to tackle.

Chapter 5

The Role of the Head

The importance of the role of the headteacher or principal in relation to innovation, briefly mentioned previously, is recognised by several writers. Hoyle (1974) observes that the headteacher has the necessary authority to introduce innovations into the school, that he has the opportunity to see the school as a whole and thus identify the need for innovation, that he controls the resources usually required by innovation and that he has contact with the 'messengers of innovation'. The headteacher is not only able to initiate innovation himself but his support is needed by an individual or group of teachers who wish to introduce an innovation. The relative autonomy of the teacher within his classroom puts considerable demands on the headteacher's leadership skills when he himself wishes to introduce an innovation. Hoyle sees the leadership role of the headteacher as an important but insufficient answer to the problems of innovation in schools.

Hoyles (1968), too, stresses the importance of the headteacher as an innovator since the education system allows him so much freedom. She states that the rate and nature of innovation depend very largely on him but that he is limited by the quality and stability of his staff. MacDonald and Rudduck (1971) also refer to the headteacher as a key figure and see him as needing to have understanding, knowledge of curriculum development in order to make appropriate choices, and also 'to be sensitive to the tensions that invariably arise in the process of innovation, and to provide for the innovating teacher a background of support without dominance' (p. 150). The headteacher's supportive role is also mentioned by several other writers (Hoyles, 1968; Richardson, 1975; Nicholls, 1979).

SUPPORT FOR INNOVATION

It was suggested earlier that innovation is frequently seen by headteachers as a single event and that once they have introduced an innovation and secured support for it they leave it in the hands of teachers. This arrangement may be regarded as a sharing of responsibility and headteachers might argue that it is both desirable and appropriate that the teachers who are to be involved in the innovation should also be associated with its development and/or implementation. They would also maintain that they provide support for the innovating teachers. In many cases this means that, as well as looking favourably on the innovation, they will help the innovating teachers in any way they can, should the teachers ask for help. Some studies of innovations have indicated that such a notion of support is insufficient for the successful implementation of complex educational innovations (Gross *et al.*, 1971; Smith and Keith, 1971; Nicholls, 1979).

In their study of a complex innovation in an elementary school in the United States, Gross and his colleagues (1971) came to the following conclusion. The starting point for an explanation of variations in the success of implementing innovations should be based on the assumption that if there is resistance to change this should be overcome as an initial prerequisite for implementation. The degree to which an innovation is implemented is a function of the extent to which five conditions are present during the period of attempted implementation. The five conditions are:

(1) There should be clear understanding of the innovation.
(2) Members of the organisation should have the capabilities necessary to carry it out.
(3) Materials and other resources should be available.
(4) Organisational arrangements should be compatible with the innovation.
(5) Staff must be willing to expend the time and effort required even if the above conditions are present.

Gross *et al.* state that the extent to which the above conditions are present is a function of the performance of management and that it is the responsibility of management to create and/or maintain these conditions.

In my own study of a complex educational innovation in a comprehensive school in the United Kingdom (Nicholls, 1979), I reached similar conclusions. I identified conditions likely to lead to successful implementation as follows:

(1) There should be a clear understanding of the innovation.
(2) The teachers should have the necessary knowledge of planning processes and the skills and abilities to develop and carry out the innovation.
(3) Criteria for the evaluation of the innovation should be stated in advance.
(4) Account should be taken of resistance to the innovation when it is identified.
(5) There should be knowledge of and attention given to the process of implementing the innovation.

(6)   Effective channels of communication should be established and
       used by all those involved with the innovation. (pp. 292–3)

In a discussion of the responsibilities of management, I suggested that
these go beyond those proposed by Gross *et al.*, namely, the creation
and/or maintenance of the conditions conducive to implementation. I
wrote:

> It is suggested that the innovator has an important task to under-
> take *before* the innovative attempts are started. This task is to carry
> out a thorough situation analysis to determine whether the condi-
> tions for likely success are present or could be established. Assum-
> ing that following the situation analysis a decision is made to
> introduce the innovation, the innovator has the further responsibil-
> ity of monitoring the innovation and providing the support and
> resources that are needed for its successful planning and
> implementation. (p. 295)

Both these views of the responsibilities of management indicate that
they extend over all phases of the life of the innovation. The conclusions of my (1979) study of a school (given the fictitious name of
Heathfield) will be discussed more fully to illustrate some issues of
importance to the role of the headteacher in relation to innovation.

The study was concerned with the initiation, planning and
implementation of a complex educational innovation, which included
the integration of some humanities subjects, unstreamed classes and
team-teaching. Although conceived initially as a single innovation,
the early division of the members of staff involved into two planning
groups resulted in the emergence of two forms of the innovation, one
of which was intended for first- and second-year pupils and the other
for third-year pupils. The life-history of the innovatory package was
described and analysed from the time of the proposal for its introduction into the school until it had been in use in the school for three
years. The problems and difficulties encountered by the staff in the
planning of the innovation were identified and it was shown that the
innovation as it was envisaged was not fully implemented. In one of
the two forms that emerged (for first- and second-years) there was a
partial implementation, while in the other (for third-years) there was
a complete lack of implementation.

Strong support for the innovation was shown by most teachers who
were in post when it was first proposed, although resistance to it was
shown later by the third-year teachers and by a newly appointed
member of staff. Resistance was considered to be a significant factor
in the lack of implementation of the innovation intended for third-
year pupils.

The manner in which the proposal for the innovation was made to the teachers was shown to be of significance although not in relation to resistance as is suggested in the literature, but rather in respect of lack of clarity about what the innovation entailed. Not only did the teachers have an unclear picture of what was involved and of their own part in the innovation, but also the headmaster whose proposal it was had no clear view. Moreover, the lack of clarity which was apparent at the outset remained throughout the period of the study. It is difficult to see how the teachers with an unclear picture of the innovation could possibly hope or be expected to play an intelligent part in its implementation.

A major problem identified in the study was a lack of relevant knowledge and abilities on the part of the teachers which manifested itself in a variety of ways. First, there was an inability to articulate certain fundamental principles related to the innovation and to identify the practical implications of these in terms of classroom practices. In particular these were concerned with integration, team-teaching and unstreamed classes. This lack of ability contributed to the persistent lack of clarity about the innovation which in turn contributed to the failure to implement it properly. There was also a lack of knowledge and ability on the part of the teachers in the approach to curriculum planning which they tried to use. This manifested itself in confusion about aims and objectives, uncertainty about the order of their planning activities, confusion about means and ends, absence of appropriate assessment techniques and a lack of structure and sequence in the course. Thirdly, the teachers placed a very heavy reliance on the use of worksheets and their lack of ability was also revealed here. Most of the tasks set for pupils were of a very low order so that pupils were unlikely to achieve many of the course objectives specified by the teachers.

It was shown that, with one exception, the teachers believed both forms of the innovation to be successful and were in favour of their continuance in the school. The teachers' judgements of success were entirely subjective and there was no provision for any formative evaluation of the innovation. The teachers' emotional involvement and the commitment of considerable time, energy and effort, together with the absence of criteria of evaluation, inhibited the identification of weaknesses or deficiencies in the innovation. Changes made to the innovation over the period of the study were minor and superficial and were mainly concerned with the improvement of presentation.

One of the two forms of the innovation which was developed displayed none of the characteristics that were initially envisaged and therefore in this form the innovation was not implemented at all. Attempts were made during the course of the study to bring it closer to the original intentions but these attempts failed because of the resistance of some of the teachers involved. The early division of the teachers into two planning groups was one factor which permitted this form of the innovation to develop. The headmaster knew that he lacked the wholehearted support of one teacher for the innovation as it was envisaged, but he did not deal with this at the outset, and the formation of two planning groups gave the teacher greater opportunity to deviate from the initial intentions.

The inadequacy of communication among the innovating teachers and between them and the headmaster was identified as an important problem. Ineffective communication was a factor in the lack of clarity about major dimensions of the innovation, which in turn affected implementation. It was also a factor related to the teachers' lack of knowledge and to the absence of any attempts to cope with resistance to the innovation.

Throughout the study the teachers involved gave all their attention to the innovation itself and devoted no time to any consideration of the actual processes of planning or implementation of the innovation. Two consequences would appear to follow from this. First, it seems likely that the innovation will become a permanent feature in the school, partly because of the effort put into its development and the teachers' commitment to it and partly because of the absence of any objective evaluation procedures. Secondly, in spite of their involvement over a period of almost four years the teachers did not appear to have learned how to plan and manage change. In other words, they had not identified principles or practices which they could apply or use in relation to another innovation.

I also discussed the role of the headmaster in relation to the innovation. The proposals for the innovation came from him; he presented his ideas about it to the teachers in a brief paper and at two meetings, but he had not worked it out clearly himself; he set up two planning groups to plan the innovation and left them to get on with the work. He asked for samples of the course to be shown to him and he made very few alterations to these. It has been suggested that his knowledge of curriculum planning may not have been great. In retrospect he was able to see that he had made mistakes in the way he introduced and managed the innovation. It would appear that there were two major deficiencies in his strategy for change. First, he failed to analyse sufficiently the situation into which he wished to introduce a particularly complex innovation. He took no steps to ascertain whether the members of staff who were to be involved had a clear understanding of the innovation and of the practical implications associated with it, or whether they had the necessary knowledge, skills and abilities to plan it and to carry it out. Additionally, in wishing to stimulate innovations throughout the school, he gave complete responsibility to the humanities teachers for this particular innovation. In trying to promote widespread innovation in his school, he failed to monitor and support sufficiently the humanities innovation. The effects of these deficiencies were that the teachers were put into the position of having to plan and develop an innovation about which they were unclear and for which they were lacking certain knowledge and skills. In spite of tremendous effort and considerable goodwill towards the innovation, difficulties arose, some of which they did not recognise and some of which they appeared to be unable to resolve. The headmaster was not aware of or did not recognise some of the difficulties and was not able to resolve the problem of resistance shown by some teachers.

These findings led to the proposal of a number of conditions which are likely to prove helpful in the promotion of innovation and which were outlined earlier (see p. 48 above). It is not claimed that the presence of this set of conditions will ensure the successful planning and implementation of an innovation, but it *is* suggested that success is more likely if the conditions exist. There are a number of practical implications related to the creation and/or maintenance of these conditions which the headteacher or principal needs to consider.

Those initiating innovations in schools need to recognise the complexities of most educational innovations. Many involve teachers in fundamental changes in their traditional roles which may cause feelings of insecurity which can sometimes reveal themselves as resistance to the innovation. Many teachers might not be able to make the changes without some forms of re-educative activity. This was shown to be the case in the study of Heathfield. It was also shown that the complexities of the innovation demanded knowledge, skills and abilities which the teachers did not have. It is necessary to recognise that the act of initiating or introducing an innovation, even when it is accepted willingly by teachers, is insufficient. Development and implementation of an innovation are both processes which need to be monitored and supported throughout. At Heathfield School the headmaster, for what to him were good reasons, initiated the innovation and then gave full responsibility for its planning and implementation to the teachers, so that he was unaware of the difficulties they encountered. In proposing an innovation, the innovator should have a clear picture of what it entails so that he can impart this to the teachers involved. It was shown in this study that the headmaster had an unclear view of the innovation and so he was unable to offer clear guidelines to the staff. The teachers' initial unclear picture was never clarified and this meant that they experienced difficulties in planning and implementation. An innovator cannot assume that if he produces an outline idea for an innovation the teachers who are to be involved necessarily have the capabilities to fill it in.

Some resistance to a proposed innovation might exist or it might develop during the process of planning or implementation. Resistance to the innovation was shown at Heathfield, was not properly dealt with and was still present at the end of the study. Resistance shown by the third-year planning group resulted in the development of a course which bore little resemblance to the original concept. The resistance shown by the newly appointed teacher to the first- and second-year course resulted in strained personal relationships and in his exclusion from planning activities. Gross *et al.* suggest that overcoming resistance is an initial prerequisite for implementation and I do not disagree with this but also take the view that the grounds for resistance should be carefully examined by the innovator since resistance can have its positive aspects. At Heathfield School if the first- and second-year group of teachers had been willing to listen to and seriously consider this teacher's views both the innovation and personal relationships in the group might have been improved. A particularly important condition and one which might be the most difficult to establish is the creation of effective channels of communications both among teachers and between them and the headteacher. It was shown in this study that there was inadequate communication about major dimensions of the innovation, about the teachers' reservations or fears and about the conflicting views of an individual and a group. It would appear to be important to create a climate in which it is quite acceptable to bring into the open and to admit to colleagues doubts, fears, or inabilities, and in which conflicting viewpoints can be discussed frankly. Many innovations are likely to generate doubts, feelings of insecurity and differing viewpoints and if these are not brought out and examined so that help or reassurance can be given and perhaps adjustments of views made, problems are likely to develop which will adversely affect the innovation. It should be recognised, however, that the creation of such an atmosphere might be extremely difficult in some schools and could constitute an innovation in itself. This matter is discussed in more detail in the following chapter.

The condition concerning evaluation implies that teachers have to face the possibility that an innovation might not be successful or only partially successful and that changes to it might have to be made. This could be a difficult possibility to face since there has often been a great commitment of time, energy and effort to an innovation, plus an emotional involvement and sometimes even career expectations. However, formative evaluation would increase the possibility that the energy, efforts and commitment were directed towards a profitable end rather than misdirected. In the longer term, attention to evaluation might lead to a situation in which the mark of an innovative school was not the number of innovations it adopted but rather the extent to which it undertook the testing of new ideas and practices and retained only those for which there was sufficient positive evidence.

The conditions which suggest that teachers might profitably pay attention to the process of curriculum planning and of implementation of innovations are predicated on the assumption that innovations are likely to be a permanent feature of teachers' professional activities. Teachers who learn principles from their involvement in one innovation which can be applied to other innovations are likely to become more expert in this field. In this study the teachers paid only superficial attention to the process of curriculum planning and the problems they experienced have been described. No attention at all was given to a strategy for the implementation of the innovation. They did not appear to have derived from their experience with this particular innovation principles related to planning and implementation which they could apply in a professional life of continuous adaptive change.

The suggested set of conditions implies that considerable time may have to be allowed for innovative attempts. The amount of time necessary will vary according to the needs of particular schools and possibly according to the complexity of the innovation. Even before the actual innovative attempts begin, time is needed for the innovator to carry out his analysis of the situation.

Analysis would be concerned first with an examination of the extent to which the proposed innovation is congruent with the overall purposes of the school and then with an assessment of the extent to which the proposed conditions exist or can be created. The analysis is likely to indicate how much time might have to be spent on such activities as planning, reading, discussion, developing knowledge and understanding of principles related to the innovation and of principles related to planning and implementation. Time may be required also for a range of re-educative activities.

To suggest that the set of conditions I have proposed should operate in a school in order to increase the possibility of the successful implementation of an innovation is to emphasise both the complexities and difficulties which confront teachers who wish to or are required to innovate, and the responsibility of headteachers to face up to the difficult task of creating and/or maintaining the conditions. This raises the question of whether all schools are able to cope with the installation of complex innovations without some form of outside help.

While the creation and maintenance of the proposed set of conditions are likely, on the one hand, to make innovations more successful, they are also likely, on the other hand, to make the task of innovating more difficult. The evidence from the Heathfield study leads me to the view that many schools would be likely to benefit from some external help and support. So much knowledge, so many abilities and skills are needed to carry out the range of activities associated with the planning and implementation of many innovations that they are unlikely all to be present in any one school, and contributions might usefully come from colleges, polytechnics, universities, local education authorities, teachers' centres and other schools. To call in outside help and support is not common practice in schools, and considerable changes in attitude would have to take place before this could happen on a voluntary basis. An important factor identified in this study and seen elsewhere was the inability of the teachers to recognise their own shortcomings and to identify problems so that they would not have known where and when they needed help even had it been available. This suggests the possibility of an external consultant from the outset who is able to recognise what help is needed and when it is needed and who is in a position to provide the help either personally or by calling in someone else. While teachers might benefit from assistance in many aspects of an innovation, it is suggested that evaluation is an area in which an outside consultant might prove to be particularly valuable. The emotional involvement and heavy commitment of time, energy and effort to an innovation make it extremely difficult for those teachers involved to stand back and make an objective evaluation. The reluctance of teachers to carry out objective evaluation was noted in the Heathfield study and is also generally recognised.

The use of outside consultants by teachers does not imply an imposition of ideas or practices from outside. The suggestion is that consultants are called upon to help teachers to examine, plan and implement the innovations they wish to introduce into their schools. However, whatever the role of an external consultant might be and however clearly this might be defined, it may well be seen to impinge on the role of the headteacher and it may require a headteacher to have considerable self-confidence and professional maturity in order for him not to feel that his own position is threatened by the use of an external consultant or change agent.

If a headteacher and his staff decide to call on such external support there are a number of related issues which require careful consideration if the exercise is not to prove frustrating to all concerned. A very important consideration concerns the fundamental role of the consultant. Is he, for instance, coming in to help the staff solve a problem that they have already identified? Or, is he coming in to help identify the initial problem and then to help solve it? It is in the interests of both parties involved that the limits and scope of the consultancy are clearly identified. It also needs to be made clear at the outset with whom final responsibility for making decisions lies. In most cases, this would be within the school. In order to save time and to help him carry out his task more efficiently the consultant needs to be well briefed about conditions within the school. This may well raise questions about how much information a headteacher feels able to give to an outside person. On the one hand there are matters of confidentiality and on the other there are the responsibilities to the consultant.

Just as it is important that the consultant should be adequately briefed about the school, so is it important that the staff should be made fully aware of what has been agreed and what is likely to take place. It is likely that it will be the headteacher who makes the arrangements with a consultant, and even if the staff agreed initially to the use of a consultant they are likely to feel apprehensive and uncertain about the exercise. These feelings could easily be transformed into opposition in the absence of knowledge of what was going to happen. Besides this, teachers need to know in order to reduce the chances of the development of misunderstandings as the consultancy proceeds. The exercise is likely to be delicate enough without the addition of problems created by ignorance.

The use of consultants in schools is not a simple matter and there is very little experience of it in the United Kingdom; it is well established in the United States. Drawing on experience from both sides of the Atlantic, Bell (1979) discusses some of the implications of using consultants in school, concentrating on the relationship between the client and the consultant. He raises a number of important issues, one of which might serve as a useful guideline for client and consultant. He writes:

> Both client and consultant have to be aware that the consultancy process confers rights and responsibilities on all of the parties involved in it, although the literature tends to concentrate on the rights of the client and the responsibilities of the consultant. The other aspects are equally important to both parties, especially if the client is to use the services of the consultant in the most effective way. (p. 57)

DECISION-MAKING

A central issue in a school that is affected by and is initiating innovation is the creation of a style of leadership which is effective in terms of managing such a complex organisation and which also takes account of the views and opinions of those who are teaching there. Bernbaum (1976) suggests that it is possible to argue for a model of the role of the headteacher which differs from the model which has predominated in the immediate past, and he puts forward two alternatives:

It can be argued that the changed conditions, especially in the large comprehensive schools, require heads who may be skilled and trained administrators capable of a kind of scientific and detailed control of the decision-making processes. Others, however, may reject such a view in favour of a non-directive role for the head, who, it is argued, cannot possibly be the essentially dominant figure of the past. In particular, it is suggested that the head should recognise the rights and potential power of the teaching staff to whom more control should be given. (p. 22)

A study by Hughes (1976) suggests two dimensions of the secondary school headteacher's role: a traditional (or local) role and an innovating (or cosmopolitan) role. The first dimension is characterised by the headteacher's regular teaching commitment and his pastoral relation to and personal involvement with both members of staff and pupils. The innovating dimension, which indicates an openness to external professional influences, is characterised, according to Hughes, by 'the head's readiness to take the initiative in getting staff to try out new ideas and media; the head's involvement in educational activities outside his own school; the importance attached to the head finding time for personal study' (p. 55).

Within each dimension a headteacher might have a high or low rating and this leads to the typology in Figure 5.1.

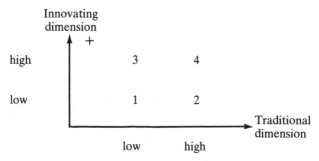

Figure 5.1 The role of the headteacher.

The four categories can be described as follows:

(1) The abdicator – below average in personal teaching and pastoral emphasis and in openness to external professional influences.
(2) The traditionalist – above average in personal teaching and pastoral emphasis but below average in openness to external professional influences.

(3) The innovator – below average in personal teaching and pastoral emphasis but above average in openness to external professional influences.
(4) The extended professional – above average in personal teaching and pastoral emphasis and in openness to external professional influences.

The headteacher's style of leadership determines the kind of authority structure that prevails in schools and Nevermann (1974) identifies four types:

(1) The authoritarian/bureaucratic type in which the principal takes decisions autocratically in a hierarchical organisation.
(2) The consultative type in which the principal retains final authority though he delegates more and uses consultative procedures.
(3) The collegial type in which authority rests with the professional staff, the principal acting as an executive, and in which pupils and parents may be consulted.
(4) The full participatory type in which authority rests with professional staff, students and perhaps parents and non-professional staff.

This clarification of the concept of participation relates to the points made in the previous chapter about the need for the terms of reference of staff groups and committees to be made quite clear if ill-feeling is not to be generated. This view is shared by Peters (1966) who, after commenting on the difficulty of establishing the machinery for consultation, writes:

> But the terms on which others are being consulted should be made clear ... Is this a situation where a meeting is summoned so that the headmaster may seek advice which perhaps he will not take? Or is it a meeting at which what is decided is going to be done? ... Rationality requires not a haphazard summoning of retainers for 'advice and consent' but a structured situation in which people know where they stand. (p. 311)

Decisions by a headteacher about the sharing or delegation of responsibility for decision-making and the retention of power to make decisions himself require very fine judgement, and whatever decisions are made are open to misinterpretation by others. The problem is well stated by Richardson (1975):

> It seems that there can be no release from the problem of making judgements, in the face of continually changing situations, about

when to retain and when to delegate power to make decisions. Failure to delegate authority is easily identifiable as autocracy or dictatorship. But the handing over of more and more authority to others can just as easily be identified as abdication. The head must preserve a precarious balance between trusting people to do their jobs and providing the supportive framework within which they can function. (p. 104)

In relation to innovation, part of the solution to the extent of delegation and shared responsibility may well lie in the nature of the supportive framework which the headteacher provides. Both Richardson (1975) and Hoyles (1968) refer to the headteacher as a teacher of teachers, while studies of innovation previously mentioned stress the need for appropriate support from those in authority (Gross *et al.*, 1971; Nicholls, 1979).

Responsibility for running a school rests with the headteacher and it is for him to decide whether he wishes to share his responsibility with his colleagues and, if so, to determine the bases for sharing. Of the three types of authority structure described by Nevermann (1974) which involve shared responsibility, the full participatory type is most rare. Even the collegial type is uncommon, and it is probably the consultative type that would be favoured by most headteachers who are willing to delegate (although not necessarily by teachers). However, a headteacher who wants innovation in his school and who wants a greater involvement of his staff in decision-making in the expectation of facilitating innovation may well face some practical problems. This was the case for the headmaster of Heathfield School. His problems serve to raise issues which may be of relevance to other headteachers in a similar situation.

He wanted innovation in his school and he genuinely wanted a greater involvement of his staff in decision-making. In preparation for the creation of the new comprehensive school he prepared a document on school organisation which very clearly gave considerable responsibilities and involvement to his staff. However, even after three years he was disappointed in the extent to which the staff accepted this sharing of responsibility. His desire for the active participation of the staff in decision-making and the production of new ideas did not materialise. There appeared to be a number of reasons for this state of affairs.

In common with other human beings, the headmaster displayed inconsistencies of behaviour which resulted in his style of management precluding the achievement of his twin objectives – innovation and staff involvement. For instance, there seemed to be an inconsistency between his apparent autocratic or power-coercive stance in the way he initiated the innovation and what appeared to be a *laissez-*

faire attitude towards the planning groups. However, behaviour which appeared to be autocratic or power-coercive might not entirely have been intended to be so. While he acknowledged that there was an element of power-coercion in his innovation strategy, he was very much a rational man and his strategy was mainly empirical-rational. He appeared to be very firmly convinced of the effectiveness of argument.

Another difficulty was that he was the main source of ideas in the school. Although his teachers supported him in many ways, they did not produce many proposals for innovation. Not only did this impose a considerable burden on him, but it also meant that he was perceived by his staff as a man with firm ideas who liked to see these ideas put into practice. Although he would have welcomed their ideas, those staff who had some proposals felt that because he had so many ideas of his own he would not want to consider theirs.

Perhaps this was a deficiency in communication as much as anything else (an issue to be disucssed fully in the next chapter) and indeed the problem of inadequate communication manifested itself in another matter related to the staff involvement. This was the headmaster's document on school organisation which reflected his concern that staff should be actively involved in decision-making and was, at the same time, an example of his foresight, his attention to detail, his tremendous hard work, and also his problem of communicating with members of staff. The document was lengthy and it contained concepts and language unfamiliar to most of the teachers but it was not discussed in any detail and so, even if read, was not fully understood. It was not surprising, therefore, that the teachers did not fill the roles envisaged by the headmaster.

There are two other issues related to the proposals for staff involvement embodied in this document. First, while the document indicated very clearly his wishes for active staff participation, it also reflected his control over decision-making processes in that he prepared the document totally unaided and without any staff discussion of the ideas expressed in it. Secondly, it appeared that the staff were expected to assume these new roles which involved participation without any form of support or help.

This was true also of their involvement in the planning and implementation of the innovation: the headmaster's approach in delegating responsibility for the innovation was quite consistent with his general approach to the authority structure in the school as outlined in his document on school organisation. However, in respect of both of the innovation and of their new roles in the authority structure, he did not establish whether the staff had the necessary knowledge and capabilities to do what he expected of them. In failing to monitor closely what they were doing he was unaware of the problems they experienced.

Although the headmaster wanted active staff participation in decision-making, in his desire to promote innovation he did not always engage in genuine consultation with his staff. Like the headteachers in Dickinson's (1975) study, while he left matters related to the method of implementation and administrative arrangements to his staff, he made all the decisions about the justification and relevance of the innovation.

This perhaps typifies the dilemma facing the innovating headteacher who wants the active involvement of his staff. Unless he makes decisions about innovation there is unlikely to be much innovation, but the more decisions he makes the less he is perceived by his staff as being willing to share decision-making with them.

The major issues related to the role of the headteacher and innovation discussed in this chapter – support for innovation, with or without the use of external consultants, and participative decision-making – may present the innovating headteacher with a fundamental problem. The type of support outlined, especially if an external consultant is used, and staff participation in decision-making are not widespread in schools; and if they are to be introduced they may constitute, in many situations, major innovations in themselves. This then means two innovations will be introduced simultaneously. Undoubtedly, this may well put great pressure on those involved, but it is likely to be worthwhile in the long term.

Chapter 6

The Setting for Innovation

It is generally accepted that in spite of having many characteristics in common no two schools are identical nor do they function in identical ways. It is not surprising, therefore, that innovations developed outside the school meet very different fates in different schools. The relative lack of impact on schools of such bodies as the Schools Council has led to a current emphasis on school-based innovation. Here again, however, schools manifest considerable differences. Some are noted for their ability to develop and implement innovations successfully, while others show little or no interest in innovation and yet others try to innovate but fail.

A fundamental problem which schools, like other organisations, face is that they establish structures and procedures necessary for their maintenance, but there are occasions when they need to innovate and frequently the established structures and procedures prove to be inappropriate for innovation. In fact, at one and the same time a school may have both to maintain existing practices and to innovate. What is it that enables some schools to carry out these two functions successfully while others seem able only to maintain themselves?

It is suggested that certain factors in the organisation determine the extent to which it is able to innovate successfully. In other words, the social context in which individuals operate may influence their innovative response. Four factors considered to be important in relation to the fostering of innovation in schools will be discussed in this chapter: organisational arrangements, school climate, organisational health and communication.

ORGANISATIONAL ARRANGEMENTS

The importance of relationships between organisational arrangements and innovations has been emphasised by several writers (Gross *et al.*, 1971; Hoyle, 1974; Hamilton, 1975; Nicholls, 1979). The way in which a school, a department, or a class is organised is not an end in itself but rather is intended to bring about desired aims and objectives. It is, therefore, essential to scrutinise organisational arrangements to ascertain whether they are facilitating or hindering innovations. Organisational arrangements that can influence innovations may be relatively minor and obvious, for instance, timetabling, rooming and examination arrangements, or more major and fundamental, for instance, delegation of responsibility and channels of communication. Even minor arrangements can have significant adverse effects on innovations and although they may be obvious to an outside observer they are frequently overlooked by those closely involved in innovations.

Both Hamilton (1975) and Nicholls (1979) noted a mismatch between the objectives of the innovation and the examination and/or assessment arrangements actually used and the school report, which resulted in a range of unintended effects. It might seem obvious that to test only the acquisition of knowledge and understanding when the curriculum had a wider range of objectives would lead to a distortion, and yet this was overlooked by the teachers in both these studies. Hamilton's study focuses on the learning milieu of an innovation and raises questions about possible tensions and mismatches between an innovation and such major factors as student grouping, department structures and decision-making machinery, as well as the relatively minor mismatch just mentioned.

One of the recommendations emerging from the study of Cambire by Gross *et al.* (1971) is that organisational arrangements should be compatible with the innovation. They found that practices that were not compatible remained unchanged during attempts to implement the innovation and this constituted one of the barriers to successful implementation.

In my study of Heathfield (Nicholls, 1979) I also found that the organisational arrangements had an adverse effect on the innovation (in addition to the examination arrangements). The fact that the school was in two buildings, some three miles apart, was at the root of the problem, but that situation was one which could not be altered. The decision to divide the school into a lower and upper school was a reasonable one, and followed the pattern of many other comprehensive schools faced with the problem of two buildings some distance apart. It was the details of timetabling and allocation of staff within the humanities faculty which contributed to certain problems.

One problem was related to the form of the innovation for third-year pupils who were based in the upper school. This form of the innovation deviated in all its major characteristics from those initially agreed. The head of the humanities faculty spent all his teaching time in the lower school with first- and second- year pupils even though he had overall responsibility throughout the school for humanities subjects. This arrangement meant that his contacts with his heads of departments and members of staff based in the upper school were minimal and his influence over them slight. This was particularly important in relation to the deviant form of the innovation since both the headmaster and the head of faculty were anxious to bring it closer to the initial concept of the innovation. The main issue of disagreement concerned integration of subjects and while it is unlikely that greater contact between the head of faculty and those teachers whose views were strongly held would have resulted in any change of opinion on their part, he might have had some success through greater contact with those teachers involved who were not strongly opposed to integration but nevertheless supported the strong opposition of other teachers. It is possible that he might have secured some measure of compliance if not total consensus. Moreover, there was some evidence of unharmonious personal relationships associated with the professional disagreement and the presence of the head of faculty in the upper school could have helped to avoid these.

The other problem concerned teachers who worked together to plan and teach the innovation in the lower school. Three of the teachers, including the head of faculty, spent most of their working time together and very strong group cohesion developed. They appeared to derive both social and professional satisfaction from working together and group membership seemed to be particularly significant to them. They taught in the same team and spent considerable time together in course development. In both facets of their work they had excellent and harmonious working relationships and they willingly undertook an enormous burden of work. This strong group feeling also had a negative aspect. Another member of the team spent most of his time in the upper school and was highly critical of the innovation. His criticisms were known to his colleagues but it appeared that they were simply dismissed; they were certainly not discussed. The reaction of the other teachers was to ignore the critic as much as possible as far as planning was concerned and to make decisions without him. While it cannot be claimed that organisational arrangements were the main factor in the problems that arose between this teacher and his three colleagues, it would appear that the near, if not complete, isolation of the three colleagues in the lower school contributed to their strong group cohesion and their close-minded attitude and total rejection of their colleague's views.

In this particular example the organisational arrangements were new since they came about in the course of the establishment of a new comprehensive school and it is possible that some careful forethought could have helped to avoid the problems that arose. However, as Hoyle (1974) points out, some major educational innovations necessitate a change in existing organisational arrangements and this can constitute an innovation in itself. In such a case a school can face a task of great complexity and difficulty. There may be instances where the two, that is, the original innovation and the organisational rearrangements, have to be carried out simultaneously, and this will put great demands on those involved. In other instances it may be possible to make the organisational changes first and then to embark on the innovation. It is worth remembering that if the organisational changes require teachers to undertake new roles, adequate time must be allowed for this and in the meantime there may be a period of temporary inefficiency (Stinchcombe, 1965).

The implication for the managers of innovation of the relationship between organisational arrangements and innovation is that they should regard school, department and classroom organisation as flexible and dynamic, not fixed and rigid, and that they should therefore be alert to the effects of these factors and be prepared to modify them when necessary.

SCHOOL CLIMATE

Visitors going into schools often make generalised statements about a school's climate based on factors they observe such as pupils' attitudes to each other, relationships between staff and between staff and pupils, and attitudes to work. A more scientific study of organisational climate was carried out by Halpin (1966) and the classification he derived from his study has been used in relation to the innovativeness of schools (Hughes, 1968).

Halpin based his study on a questionnaire he devised, the Organisational Climate Description Questionnaire, which is concerned with administrative relationships in schools. Factorial analysis of the data from responses to the questionnaires revealed eight major dimensions, four relating to staff behaviour and four to the principal's behaviour. Further analysis indicated that these dimensions could be classified into six major clusters, each of which could be used to depict a different type of organisational climate, which Halpin ranged in order from open to closed, an open climate being characterised by flexibility and a closed climate by rigidity. The six climates are summarised as follows:

(1) *Open*
    There is a high level of morale and teachers work well together. Their tasks are facilitated by the principal's policies. Group members enjoy friendly relations but do not feel the need for a high degree of intimacy. The principal sets a good example by working hard and he either criticises or helps teachers according to the circumstances. He provides subtle direction and control but does not monitor the work of his staff too closely. He is in full control and provides leadership for the staff.

(2) *Autonomous*
    The principal gives almost complete freedom to the staff to provide their own structures. There tends to be more emphasis

on satisfying social needs than on task achievement. Teachers work well together and accomplish the tasks of the organisation. Morale is high. The principal remains aloof and runs the school in a rather impersonal manner. He does not personally check that teachers are getting things done and lets them work at their own speed. He sets an example and works hard himself. He has sufficient flexibility to maintain control and to be concerned with the personal welfare of teachers.

(3) *Controlled*

The emphasis here is on achievement at the expense of satisfaction of social needs. There is high morale and teachers get on with the job. There is an excessive amount of paper-work and few procedures exist to facilitate their work. The principal is authoritarian and controls his staff closely. He is aloof and cares little about people's feelings.

(4) *Familiar*

The main feature of this climate is the friendly relations between principal and teachers. The emphasis is on satisfaction of social needs at the expense of task achievement. The principal exerts little control or direction and is concerned to keep a happy family atmosphere.

(5) *Paternal*

This climate is characterised by the principal's ineffective attempts to control the teachers as well as to satisfy their social needs. The teachers do not work well together and do not enjoy good relations and have given up trying. The principal is everywhere and becomes intrusive, wanting to do everything himself. The school is his main interest in life, but he fails to motivate his staff mainly because he does not provide an example or an ideal which they wish to emulate.

(6) *Closed*

Group members obtain little satisfaction in either task achievement or social needs. The principal is ineffective in guiding their activities and not inclined to consider their personal welfare. Morale is low and teachers do not work well together. The principal is aloof and impersonal and does not motivate his teachers. He does not provide adequate leadership.

In an American study of 'most innovative' and 'least innovative' school districts using Halpin's questionnaire, it was found that the most innovative districts were more similar to the open climate, were less disengaged (that is, more task-oriented) and higher on *esprit* (that is, their social needs were being satisfied and they enjoyed a sense of accomplishment). The least innovative districts, when compared with the most innovative, were more similar to the closed climate, more disengaged and lower on *esprit*. The leader (in this case the superintendent) in innovative districts showed more thrust, that is, he was highly motivated and led more by example than by issuing orders (Hughes, 1968). However, the findings of Hughes's research suggest that 'only certain aspects of organisational climate may be related to innovativeness' (p. 23).

Using a different measure of organisational climate, another study (Hilfiker, 1970) also found a relationship between innovativeness and openness (characterised by ready accessibility, co-operative attitudes, tolerance of internal change and permissiveness of diversity in social situations) and trust (the degree to which an individual perceives interpersonal relationships as characterised by an assured reliance or confident dependence on the character, ability, or truthfulness of others).

ORGANISATIONAL HEALTH

A very similar concept is that of organisational health which is discussed widely in the literature and is considered to be closely related to innovativeness. One of the early comments on organisational health sees it as the organisation's continuing ability to cope with change and to adapt to the future (Kubie, 1958). A similar view is that which sees an organisation as being healthy if it produces behaviour which 'allows all levels of the organisation to meet two basic but diverse requirements – maintenance of the status quo and growth' (Clark, 1969, p. 282).

Miles (1965) has developed a view of organisational health which relates specifically to schools. He defines it as 'the school system's ability not only to function effectively, but to develop and grow into a more fully-functioning system' (p. 12). He argues that this aspect of innovation has been neglected in the past and yet, in his view, attention to it is likely to reveal more than anything else about the probable success of any particular innovative efforts. Miles's conceptualisation of organisational health has ten dimensions:

(1) *Goal focus*
    According to Miles, in a healthy organisation not only would the goals of the system be reasonably clear to the members and reasonably well accepted by them, but they would also be achievable and appropriate.
(2) *Communication adequacy*
    This characteristic of organisational health suggests, in Miles's terms, that there is 'relatively distortion-free communication "vertically", "horizontally", and across the boundary of the system to and from the surrounding environment' (p. 18).

(3) *Optimal power equalisation*

Miles puts the argument that in a healthy organisation the distribution of influence is relatively equitable, that where there is a formal hierarchical structure subordinates can influence upwards and they perceive that their boss can influence his boss.

(4) *Resource utilisation*

Miles is referring here particularly to human resources and he sees a healthy organisation as one in which there is little feeling of strain, since although people may be working hard they are not working against themselves or the organisation. People see themselves as learning, growing and developing as persons as they make their contributions to the organisation.

(5) *Cohesiveness*

By this, Miles means that members feel attracted to be part of the organisation, that they want to stay with it, that they want to be influenced by it and that they want to exert their influence over it in a collaborative manner.

(6) *Morale*

Miles acknowledges that there are problems in the social-psychological field associated with this concept, yet he argues that it is a useful notion at the organisational level. He defines morale as 'a summated set of individual sentiments, centering around feelings of well-being satisfaction and pleasure, as opposed to feelings of discomfort, un-wished-for strain and dissatisfaction' (p. 20). To a limited extent morale is related to cohesiveness, in the same sense that if members are attracted to an organisation and wish to stay with it morale is likely to be high.

(7) *Innovativeness*

A healthy organisation, according to Miles, is capable of growing developing and changing, rather than remaining routinised and standard.

(8) *Autonomy*

Miles argues that a healthy organisation would respond neither passively nor destructively or rebelliously to demands from the environment but rather that, it would have a kind of independence. Schools should respond to the needs of their environment but not to such an extent that demands from outside become the determinants of what takes place within them. This view sees teachers as having a clear and well-understood statement of goals which, in their formulation, have taken into account the needs of the society in which the school is functioning. Demands or pressures from the environment can then be considered within this overall framework rather than being accepted meekly or rejected defiantly.

(9) *Adaptation*

This dimension concerns the ability of an organisation to cope with required changes. A healthy organisation would need to have sufficient stability and tolerance in the face of stress to cope with the difficulties that occur during the process of adaption.

(10) *Problem-solving adequacy*

Miles is referring here to the manner in which an organisation copes with problems. A healthy organisation has, as he puts it, 'well-developed structures, and procedures for sensing the existence of problems, for inventing possible solutions, for implementing them, and for evaluating their effectiveness' (p. 21).

Several of these dimensions have been identified elsewhere in this book as factors likely to be important in the successful implementation of innovations. Goal focus is related to the condition concerning the need for a clear understanding of innovations proposed by Gross *et al.*, (1971) and Nicholls (1979). Communication adequacy is another condition proposed by Nicholls and is discussed fully below, while Miles's problem-solving adequacy is very similar to Nicholls's concern for knowledge of and attention to the processes of planning and implementation. The dimensions of optimal power equalisation and cohesiveness have points in common with the ideas for participative decision-making discussed earlier, while the notion of autonomy is similar to the point mentioned previously that systematic planning enables a considered response to be made to the demands of society and provides schools with a way to resist being overwhelmed by them.

There is, however, disagreement about the basic concept of organisational health, not to mention its utility in relation to innovation or to the possibility of changing the organisational health of a school. The concept of the health of an organisation would be criticised, for example, by those who hold a phenomenologist view and by those structuralists who take a conflict perspective. In particular, the concept proposed by Miles is criticised by Stenhouse (1975). There is no body of empirical evidence to support its usefulness, although aspects of the studies of Cambire and Heathfield provide some support for some of the dimensions, as indicated above.

In discussing the implications of his own research, Hilfiker (1970) makes a point in agreement with Miles, namely, that little attention has been given to the social or psychological characteristics of schools and how these characteristics might affect the fate of an innovation. He believes that the long-term success of innovative efforts may be due to a greater degree than has been thought, to the social-psychological state of the school's climate. He continues as follows:

> If it becomes possible to consistently diagnose and evaluate the 'state' of a school system's organizational climate, it might be feasible to modify the adaptability of professional personnel and to change or create organizational structures and processes which tend to enhance the possibilities of successful institutionalization of innovations. (p. 27)

Halpin (1967), reviewing research on school climates, states that it is not yet known how to change a climate. However, Schmuck and Miles (1971), discussing Miles's concept of organisational health, argue that it is possible to improve organisational health through the application of organisational development strategies, and they describe cases where this approach has been used successfully.

One factor that might contribute to this difference of viewpoint is that there is a significant difference between Halpin's concept of school climate and Miles's concept of organisational health. In the former the concern is entirely with people – the principal and his staff – their relationships, behaviour and attitudes, whereas in the latter the emphasis is on features of the organisation. It is more difficult to change the former than the latter and less is known about how to do it. However, it must not be overlooked that in changing features of an organisation, changes in people must also take place.

The fact that one emphasises people and the other features of the organisation is perhaps a reason why neither concept appears to be useful on its own as a means of assessing the innovativeness of a school, since both are important factors in innovation. Each, however, draws attention to matters which the potential innovator might be wise to consider.

Some research has shown that there is a relationship between innovativeness and an open climate. This climate is characterised by the leadership qualities of the principal; he is in full control and provides appropriate support for his teachers. It also shows that the response of the teachers is an important factor; they work well together and their morale is high. This emphasises the point made earlier that it is the interaction between a principal and his staff which is important; each party is dependent on the other for support, and the actions and attitudes of each influence those of the other.

Except in very small schools, in addition to certain qualities in both principal and staff it is likely that certain structures, processes or qualities are likely to be necessary in the school organisation if innovation is to be successful. These are not independent of those who work in the school and, indeed, can only be present in the school as a result of what the personnel in the school actually do. Attention has already been drawn to those features in Miles's conceptualisation which some studies have shown to be significant factors in successful innovation. These include goal focus, problem-solving adequacy, autonomy, optimal power-equalisation, cohesiveness and communication adequacy.

COMMUNICATION

The establishment of clear communications within an institution was one of the requirements of a healthy organisation identified by Miles. Other writers have also stressed the importance to innovation of a good communication system which works effectively both vertically and horizontally and which permits people to be heard as well as talked to.

In the study of Heathfield (Nicholls, 1979) deficiencies in the communication system emerged as a factor of considerable significance. Deficiencies existed in communication both between the headmaster and staff and, perhaps more surprisingly, among the teachers who were involved in the innovation. Communication about the innovation between the headmaster and the staff concerned began when he introduced his proposal for the innovation. Communication tended to be in one direction, from the headmaster to the staff, and that it took the form of a rather imprecise written statement and meetings chaired by the headmaster. The staff did not derive a clear picture of the innovation from these forms of communication. However, the headmaster had no reason to think that the staff were having difficulty in understanding clearly what the innovation entailed, since they did not make him aware of any difficulty. He was available for help, advice and discussion, a situation recognised by at least some members of staff, and so if difficulties or problems were not brought to his attention he was likely to assume that they did not exist. He did, however, recognise some breakdown in communications between himself and the staff when, during an interview with the investigator, he answered a question about the initial reaction of the staff to the idea of the innovation. He said that there was no overt reaction by the staff but some talk in the staffroom which he described and interpreted in the following words: 'There was a fair amount, from what I gather, of chuntering in the staffroom which seemed to indicate a breakdown in communication, rather than communications working and rejection of what was being communicated' (Nicholls, 1979, p. 281). Later in the study he acknowledged that he had not made any organised attempt to find out what the teachers' views were but relied on certain senior members of staff to provide him with this information, a procedure he recognised as lacking in accuracy.

Planning and teaching of the first- and second-year innovation was on a team basis and so the nature and extent of communication between team members was of considerable significance to the innovation. During interviews with the investigator the teachers spoke freely of their fears, concerns and uncertainties about the innovation, sometimes expressing doubts about their own ability to cope with it. There was no evidence that the teachers ever expressed these fears to each other.

Another deficiency in communication was the absence of any attempt to discuss the major dimensions of the innovation, that is, integration, team-teaching and non-streamed classes, and the implications of these for what was to take place in the classroom. Possible reasons for this lack of communication might include insufficient time, deficiencies in knowledge or an assumption of shared meanings (see Sharp and Green, 1975). Whatever the reasons, the effect was that the initial lack of clarity persisted throughout the study and was regarded by the investigator as a major factor in the failure to fully implement the innovation intended for first- and second-year pupils. It was not that the teachers did not speak freely to each other but rather that they did not discuss fundamental issues or refer to their doubts and uncertainties.

It has to be recognised that it is very difficult to create in schools the conditions and the climate in which clear, unambiguous and open communications operate, particularly when innovations are involved. Innovations involve risks, create uncertainties and doubts and include the possibility of temporary incompetence and even failure, while teachers are expected to display competence, have knowledge and be successful, especially if they are ambitious. The climate in most schools does not encourage teachers to admit to colleagues any lack of knowledge or fears about their ability to cope in a new situation. Yet, if such matters are not brought out into the open, an innovation may proceed with teachers inadequately prepared to develop and implement it, as in the Cambire and Heathfield studies.

Both these studies point to the responsibility of management to create the conditions in which innovation is more likely to be successfully implemented, but it should not be overlooked that members of staff, too, have a measure of responsibility. Communication is a two-way process and teachers need to be willing to communicate with the headteacher as well as listen to him. It was pointed out above that at Heathfield the teachers did not tell the headmaster that they had certain concerns and so he was not fully aware of their problems. The same was true at Cambire. It is a question, therefore, of all the staff in the school, including the headteacher or principal, working together to create a climate in which questions can be asked without fear of ridicule, in which admissions of concern about doubts or uncertainties can be made without fear of condemnation and in which constructive criticism of proposals can be made without fear of hostility.

Another aspect of communication that was of significance in the Heathfield study was that associated with conflict. Three instances of conflict manifested themselves during the course of the study: (1) the initial and increasing opposition to the first- and second-year course by one teacher; (2) the third-year teachers' resistance to an integrated course; (3) reported criticism of the humanities teachers based in the lower school by teachers based mainly in the upper school (the two were physically separate).

The criticisms by one member of staff of the first- and second-year course have already been mentioned. The head of the humanities faculty expressed some anxiety about this situation during interviews with the investigator but it appeared that there was a reluctance on his part to discuss the differing viewpoint with the teacher concerned. There was evidence to suggest that the head of faculty was not really sure what this viewpoint was but that he seemed to see the situation as one in which he should try to make the teacher concerned change his mind. There appeared to be no question of discussion and mutual adjustment. Throughout the period of the study, the head of faculty and the other teachers in the first- and second-year planning group ignored the dissenting teacher and continued to plan without him when it became apparent that he did not share their views.

In the case of the opposition of the third-year teachers, two meetings were held during the first and second year of the innovation in an attempt to make them change their minds about an integrated course, but there was no evidence of any continuing dialogue between these teachers and the head of faculty. By the end of the study the third-year teachers still had not agreed to develop an integrated course and the head of faculty and the headmaster were still unhappy about this.

The third area of conflict was brought to the attention of the investigator by both the headmaster and the head of faculty. Criticism was being made, mainly subversively or semi-jocularly during meetings, by staff in other departments of staff in the humanities faculty. In mentioning this, the headmaster said that he himself might be responsible to some extent for these feelings of hostility, albeit inadvertently, by his holding up of the faculty as a good example in an attempt to encourage other departments to innovate. This manifestation of conflict, therefore, was more in the nature of a by-product of the innovation, rather than something that had a direct bearing on the implementation of the innovation. It seemed to be a matter of some concern both to the headmaster and to the head of faculty and yet, as in the other instances, there was a reluctance to enter into an open discussion with the teachers concerned.

Richardson (1967) has suggested that conflict is best handled by bringing it out into the open and examining it, and McGregor (1960) makes a similar point in discussing the characteristics of an effective group. One characteristic he describes as follows:

> There is disagreement. The group is comfortable with this and shows no signs of having to avoid conflict or to keep everything on a plane of sweetness and light. Disagreements are not suppressed or overridden by premature group action. The reasons are carefully examined, and the group seeks to resolve them rather than to dominate the dissenter. (p. 233)

The first- and second-year planning group, particularly, had it been able to display this characteristic, might have avoided a situation in which one member was very unhappy and bitter and exhibited little job satisfaction, and in which the other members were uneasy about his opposition. Moreover, a careful examination of the dissenter's views might have resulted in some improvement of the innovation. Failure to establish and maintain open communication meant that conflict remained in all three areas described, two of which adversely affected the implementation of the innovation.

It is to be expected that innovation is likely to provoke conflict. Indeed, it is difficult to envisage a situation in which an innovation of any significance will not give rise to different responses from a group of thinking professionals. Conflict is unlikely to go away because it is ignored; it is not easy to deal with; at times it might even be unpleasant. However, the creation of a climate in which ideas can be discussed openly, criticised and rejected, while those putting forward the ideas are accepted within the group, is more likely to lead to successful innovation.

Another aspect of communication that is of significance to innovation is concerned with its language. Jackson's (1968) comments on teachers' language are of relevance to this point. His observations led him to this conclusion (p. 144):

> The absence of technical terms is related to another aspect of teachers' talk: its conceptual simplicity. Not only do teachers avoid elaborate words, they also seem to shun elaborate ideas ... Four aspects of the conceptual simplicity revealed in teachers' language are worthy of comment. These are:
>
> (1) an uncomplicated view of causality;

(2) an intuitive rather than rational approach to classroom events;

(3) an opinionated as opposed to an open-minded stance when confronted with alternative technique practice;

(4) a narrowness in the working definitions assigned to abstract terms.

Some of the characteristics identified by Jackson were also to be found in the humanities teachers in the Heathfield study. The absence of technical terms in their language was notable, even in planning meetings related to the innovation. They avoided any discussion of the ideas or principles underlying the innovation. Their 'opinionated stance' was evident in the third-year teachers' attitude to integration, but most evident in the first- and second-year teachers' total disregard of the views of the dissident member. In addition to the characteristics identified by Jackson there was evidence to suggest that the teachers assumed that they all meant the same thing when they spoke of such matters as team-teaching and an integrated course.

An innovation as complex as that proposed at Heathfield School demanded a level of teacher understanding and flexibility of mind that were, in practice, at variance with some of the characteristics the teachers displayed through their use of language, which was conceptually simple and lacking in precision and clarity. Educational theory has not yet reached a stage of development where technical terms have clearly understood and universally accepted meanings, and perhaps it never will, but it is of critical importance that teachers working together to plan innovation should be prepared to discuss the meaning of the ideas and principles underlying their innovations in order to establish, among other things, that they are at least talking about the same thing.

This chapter has been concerned with the setting in which innovation takes place and some of the characteristics of schools which are thought to affect the fate of innovations. The characteristics, whether they relate to climate, organisational health, channels of communication or the nature of communication, are all created by the staff who work in the schools. While it might be the headteacher or principal who has the major responsibility for creating a setting that is favourable for innovation, it is not a task he can do alone. It is one which requires a positive contribution from the staff since the characteristics identified in this chapter are largely a function of the interaction among all members of a school staff.

Chapter 7

Evaluating Innovations

Evaluation as a planned and systematic activity is probably the most neglected aspect of innovation in schools. When evaluation is carried out it tends to be highly subjective and based on intuition or general impressions. There is no unwillingness on the part of teachers to undertake assessment; the giving of marks or grades to pupils' work is one of teachers' normal daily tasks. However, the carrying out of evaluation, the making of judgements based on a range of evidence from several sources, one of which might be pupils' work, is a different matter. The studies of innovations at Cambire (Gross *et al.*, 1971), Kensington (Smith and Keith, 1971) and Heathfield (Nicholls, 1979) all revealed teachers' neglect of evaluation.

The study of fifteen schools by Dickinson (1975) showed the attitude of the headteachers to innovation. All fifteen headteachers considered the innovations in their schools to be successful but, as Dickinson points out, successful introduction of the innovation was the yardstick of success of the innovation itself and success of this type seemed to be a major aim of the schools. As Dickinson puts it: 'Real measures of evaluation in terms of learning outcomes, or understanding, appeared to be irrelevant provided the innovation was successfully brought about' (p. 147). Dickinson also notes an absence of any innovation that failed and the permanence of changes once they were initiated. These factors are closely related to the disregard of evaluation, although there might be additional reasons operating. Another significant feature of this study was that when the headteachers were asked 'In the light of your experience with this change, what would your immediate reaction be if faced with having to do it again?' fourteen responded they would do it again as before and only one considered the possibility of making modifications. The impression here is that nothing had been learned from the experience of innovating, but in the absence of evaluation this is not surprising.

Evidence from the Heathfield study will be used to show the attitudes of teachers in that school to evaluation and the practices that they employed. The teachers were asked during interviews held a year apart what changes had been made, what changes were planned, what the reasons for the changes were and what methods of evaluation had been used. Their answers were of two kinds: those that were very vague and general about changes made and planned and those that were specific and referred to changes in presentation and layout or to minor modifications in content. All the teachers used the pupils' work as the source of evidence on which to base these changes, while some teachers gave vague subjective judgements, unsupported by evidence, about pupils' attitudes to work. The teachers' use of pupils' work as the principal, if not exclusive, source of evaluation of the innovation corresponds with their view of evaluation indicated in written curriculum outlines. In these, pupils' learning activities, which were often identical with the stated objectives, were indicated as the means of evaluation.

An examination of the course materials and observation of the course in action in the classrooms indicated that the changes made, were, as the teachers stated, largely in presentation and layout or in matters of detail. Over a period of three years there were no changes of a fundamental nature and the innovation remained essentially the same. One teacher acknowledged with regret towards the end of the study that there had been no systematic evaluation. There appeared to be no distinction in the minds of the other teachers between assessment and evaluation and they did not discuss the question of evaluation at all. It is not surprising, in view of the limited attention given to evaluation, that the curriculum revision which did take place was quite superficial.

The staff at Heathfield are not alone in their relative disregard of evaluative procedures. The lack of use by teachers of a range of evaluative techniques is noted by a number of writers (as was shown above) and it has been observed that teachers tend to select from their classroom experience those events which conform to their expectations and beliefs and ignore all other events (Adams and Biddle, 1970). It is interesting to note that while independent observers' views of innovations in schools tend to be records of failure, teachers' accounts tend to be records of success. (For example, compare Gross *et al.*, 1971; Smith and Keith, 1971 and Nicholls, 1979 with Mather, 1970; Mitchell, 1972 and Moss, 1977). A disregard of systematic evaluation by teachers might be one explanation for this. It is undeniable that to engage in evaluative procedures is time-consuming which might be a factor acting as a deterrent to teachers, and it also has to be acknowledged that few teachers are knowledgeable about evaluation. However, it is an important task in the process of innovation which whatever the difficulties, needs to be tackled if schools are to become self-renewing institutions.

THE NEED FOR EVALUATION

The definition of innovation stated at the outset included the important element of improvement in relation to desired objectives. In introducing an innovation into a school teachers really should be saying that on the basis of their professional knowledge and expertise the innovation is *likely* to be an improvement but that at that stage they cannot be sure. Before and during the process of implementation evidence needs to be collected to enable teachers to make a judgement about the extent of the improvement, if any. It is unlikely that an innovation of any complexity will be all good or all bad. Some elements are likely to be an improvement on existing practice and others are not. The evidence collected, therefore, provides a basis for making changes or modifications to the innovation.

The activities of innovating are time-consuming and demand considerable effort and energy from those involved. They may also be expensive in terms of material resources. It is important that time, effort and materials should not be wasted but used productively. Evaluation can provide evidence on which to make judgements about the use of these resources.

There is often an emotional involvement of teachers in an innovation. Some teachers are very committed to an innovation with which they are involved and 'believe in' its worth. Where there is such an emotional involvement teachers are unlikely to recognise any weaknesses or deficiencies in the innovation. Smith and Keith (1971) make an interesting comment on this characteristic which they call an unassailable belief: 'An unassailable belief is an idea that is held so strongly and closely that it is unyielding to intellectual attack or analysis ... Such conviction seems to create a charisma among the staff that furthers the commitment and enthusiasm' (p. 109). It was suggested earlier that criteria for the evaluation of an innovation should be stated in advance. While this would not remove all the problems associated with emotional involvement, it might help teachers to look at the evidence a little more objectively. An emotional attachment to an innovation combined with a heavy investment of time and effort are very powerful factors operating against the possibility of rational judgements. The establishment of criteria for judgements in advance of implementation might act as a countervailing force. The identification in advance of criteria for the evaluation of an innovation does not preclude the recognition and use of other evidence that might emerge, but provides a framework of basic evidence.

It is not only the innovation itself that needs to be evaluated but also the management of the innovation. The point being made here is that the activities of innovating should be monitored and evaluated so that they can be improved for future innovation in the school. The usual practice in schools involved in innovation is for attention to be directed exclusively on the innovation and its development, while the processes of innovation tend to be ignored. This means that the opportunity is missed to improve the skills of managing innovations and to learn from the experience of innovating by identifying productive practices and eliminating unsuccessful ones. If innovating is to be part of teachers' professional responsibilities then it would seem desirable to evaluate the activities associated with innovating in order that teachers might become more proficient in them.

EVALUATION AS A PROCESS

If this wider view of evaluation is taken, namely, that it embraces both the innovation itself and the activities of innovating, then it is useful to consider evaluation as a continuous process. This means that evaluation does not take place on a single occasion at or towards the end of the period of implementation but rather that it is related to all the activities of planning, developing and implementing an innovation and that the process of evaluation matches the processes of development and management of innovation. In undertaking evaluation in this way it is a formative process with the purpose of improving both the innovation itself and its management. The notion of summative evaluation is not considered to be appropriate unless an innovation is to be discarded. The emphasis is one of constant improvement.

Evaluation of this kind begins even before a particular innovation has been identified. It begins when judgements are being made about desirability, need and feasibility in relation to innovation. Reference was made earlier to the importance of the innovator undertaking a situation analysis in order to determine, among other things, whether the conditions for likely success are present or if they could be established. This is a form of evaluation, and in the wider view of evaluation suggested here there is a merging of situation analysis and evaluation, with evaluation being seen as continuous, multi-faceted and taking place over a broad front.

WHAT IS TO BE EVALUATED

The framework suggested below offers an indication of the main focal points of an evaluation programme. It includes some of the questions that might be asked, *but it is not exclusive.* Indeed, it cannot be exclusive because evaluation needs to match both the innovation and the processes of innovation and therefore will vary in detail from one situation to another. The major dimensions of the framework include three phases: preparation (situation analysis), planning and implementation. This implies an orderly sequence from preparation to planning and implementation but in reality the exercise of evaluating during these phases, like the activities inherent in each phase, is unlikely to be carried out in such a neat and tidy manner. Since the activities in each phase are interrelated it is more likely that there will be a moving from one phase to another, and this may well be the case with evaluation.

Framework for an Evaluation Programme
(1) Preparation (Situation Analysis)
    (a) Desirability of innovating
        (i) Why are we considering innovating?
        (ii) What is the problem?
        (iii) Are we clear about our needs?
    (b) The innovation
        (i) Is there an existing innovation that suits our needs?
        (ii) If so, how and where was it developed?
        (iii) What are its aims and objectives, stated or implied?
        (iv) Are they compatible with those of the school or department?
        (v) Does it demand knowledge/skills that teachers who will be involved do not have?
        (vi) If so, can the knowledge/skills be acquired? How? Where?
        (vii) Is the innovation complex and difficult to understand?
        (viii) If so, what needs to be done to counteract this?
        (ix) Will some outside support be needed?
        (x) If so, what kind and where is it available?
        (xi) What resources, materials, specialist rooms, expense, etc. will be involved?
        (xii) In what ways might this innovation be better than what we are doing now? Is there any evidence available? Is the evidence relevant to our situation?
        (xiii) What will we accept as evidence of improvement when the innovation is in operation?
        (xiv) If there is no suitable innovation in existence, are we able to devise our own? Do we have the necessary skills and knowledge?
    (*Many of the above questions asked about an existing innovation need to be answered in relation to innovations developed in the school.*)
    (c) The setting and personnel
        (i) Is the environment/climate appropriate for innovation?
        (ii) Are the organisational arrangements appropriate for the innovation?
        (iii) Can the teachers express their views openly?

    (iv)   Do they do so?
     (v)   Are they listened to?
    (vi)   Are they keen to participate?
   (vii)   Is there likely to be any opposition?
  (viii)   Will the teachers be able to cope with the strains, pressures, problems, extra workload that might be involved?
    (ix)   What experience of innovating have they had?
     (x)   How can this be used?
    (xi)   What is the scope of this particular task of innovating? Can we cope with it? If not, what has to be done to remedy the deficiencies?
(2) Planning
  (a) Introducing the innovation
      (i)   Was the innovation explained with sufficient clarity?*
     (ii)   Were the teachers aware of potential problems as well as advantages?
    (iii)   Did we understand clearly what was involved in practical terms before we started?
    (iv)   Was enough time allowed for discussion?
     (v)   Was notice taken of objections, fears, problems?
    (vi)   Did we allow these to be fully explored?
   (vii)   Did we encourage a frank expression of these?
  (viii)   What was done to reassure the doubters?
    (ix)   Were these measures successful?
     (x)   How did the doubters eventually cope with the innovation?
    (xi)   Was there sufficient support and/or in-service training?
  (b) Processes of planning
      (i)   Was the planning sufficiently detailed and clear?
     (ii)   Was there too much planning? Were we too rigid in our approach?
    (iii)   How did we cope with the unexpected?
    (iv)   Did we give adequate attention to the means of innovating as well as to the ends?
     (v)   Was there sufficient identification of and planning for the various stages of innovation?
    (vi)   What problems arose at different stages? How were these resolved?
   (vii)   How did staff react at different stages?

* The change to the past tense at this point is because while the earlier questions form part of the situation analysis and are concerned with the present state of affairs, these questions are asked about what happened during planning.

     (viii)   What notice was taken of staff reactions?

     (ix)   Was sufficient use made of staff abilities in the sharing and allocation of tasks at different stages?

     (x)   Was there enough staff involvement?

     (xi)   Was outside help needed at any stage? If so, what kind?

     (xii)   What omissions were there?

     (xiii)   What deficiencies were noted?

     (xiv)   What mistakes were made?

     (xv)   What can be done about these?

(3) Implementation

   (a) The innovation in use

     (i)   Is the innovation working as intended? In what ways?

     (ii)   Has it been modified? How? Why?

     (iii)   Is the innovation achieving what was hoped?

     (iv)   If not, why not? If so, in what ways?

     (v)   What are the reactions of the teachers involved?

     (vi)   What are the reactions of the pupils?

     (vii)   What will be the response to these reactions?

     (viii)   What problems have arisen? How can these be overcome?

     (ix)   Were there sufficient resources? Were they appropriate? What are future needs likely to be?

     (x)   Were there unanticipated outcomes?

     (xi)   What improvements/modifications need to be made? Why?

     (xii)   Were they any organisational problems?

     (xiii)   Did the organisational arrangements match the needs of the innovation?

   (b) Evaluation

     (i)   Is the scope of the evaluation sufficiently wide?

     (ii)   Are the sources of evidence appropriate?

     (iii)   Are there weaknesses in the techniques of evaluation?

     (iv)   Is the evidence being used? In what ways?

Within this three-phase framework the desirability of innovating, the innovation, the setting and personnel, the introduction of the innovation, processes of planning, the innovation in use and evaluation itself have been identified as major focal points. The task of the evaluators is to produce evidence in answer to the questions posed about these focal points and to propose action, where necessary, on the basis of the evidence. This requires attention to be given to the means of collecting the evidence.

There is a wide range of devices and techniques that can be used; these include interviews, questionnaires, logbooks, pupils' work, observation schedules, checklists, discussions and examination of teaching materials, projects, or written courses. Clearly, to devise some of these require skills and knowledge of a high order if they are to collect evidence that is of value, and such expertise might not be available in all schools. However, this need not be a barrier to making a start on evaluation since some techniques and devices are well within the competence of most teachers and there is a large literature available to help in this task. One factor to be borne in mind is that any step that can be taken to move away from a situation in which evaluation is based on wholly superficial subjective and emotional judgements is likely to be an improvement.

WHO CARRIES OUT EVALUATION?

The usual practice, when there is any evaluation at all, is that the task is undertaken by those teachers who are involved with an innovation. While it can be argued that they are the most appropriate persons to carry out evaluation because they are fully conversant with the innovation, the reverse could also be the case. In the first place, they are likely to be emotionally involved and quite understandably, they are likely to want to see the innovation succeed. They are also likely to have expended considerable effort and energy in trying to ensure the success of the innovation and would not wish to see their investment wasted. Factors such as these can make it difficult for teachers who are closely involved with an innovation to recognise any weaknesses or deficiencies in it. Since an objective evaluation of innovations is of such crucial importance to the development of self-renewing schools it might be necessary for serious consideration to be given to alternative arrangements, whereby evaluation of innovations is carried out by people other than, or in addition to, those immediately and closely involved.

One alternative is to bring into the school an external consultant with expertise in evaluation. This arrangement would have the advantages that the consultant would be skilled and knowledgeable in evaluation and would be impartial and objective about the innovation. However, there might be problems associated with the acceptability of an outside person to teachers, particularly in the sensitive area of evaluation. Moreover, if the innovation were related to a particular curriculum area and the evaluator were not a specialist in this, teachers might be doubtful about his competence to evaluate it. This disadvantage is more likely to be perceived than real.

A second alternative is to have a teacher in the school with specialist qualifications or expertise in evaluation and to use him for the evaluation of all innovations in the school. This arrangement would have the advantages of specialist knowledge and expertise and impartiality and objectivity as in the use of the external consultant, together with the increased acceptability of a colleague. The perceived disadvantage of absence of expertise in some curriculum areas, however, would remain. This arrangement also places considerable responsibility on one person and could impose many pressures.

A third alternative, which would share this responsibility, would be for a group of teachers not involved in the innovation to be the evaluators. This would have the advantage of impartiality and objectivity but the possible disadvantages of lack of expertise in evaluation and the particular area of the curriculum.

An arrangement that brings the advantages of the alternatives mentioned and eliminates the disadvantages is one in which the tasks associated with evaluation are shared between those who are involved in the innovation and colleagues who are not. The arrangement would work best if the group were to include at least one expert in evaluation, whether this was a member of staff or an external consultant. A consultant would probably be more acceptable to teachers if he were one of a group that had a shared responsibility, rather than if he were acting in a more dominant role as in the first alternative suggested.

The sharing arrangement could work in the following manner. The programme of evaluation can be broken down into these tasks or stages: the identification of evidence to be collected and ways of collecting it; the collection of evidence; judging the evidence; proposing action on the basis of the evidence; carrying out the action. The identification of evidence and ways of collecting it would be a joint exercise between those who were involved in the innovation and those who were not. At this stage the involvement of an expert evaluator would be a great advantage. The actual collection of evidence would be undertaken by the teachers directly involved with the innovation. The next two tasks, judging the evidence and proposing appropriate action, would be carried out by the joint group, while the action would be taken by those involved.

This arrangement offers the possibility of an appropriate balance between impartiality on the one hand and detailed knowledge of an innovation on the other. It broadens the responsibility for making critical decisions about an innovation but leaves in the hands of those involved the responsibility for taking action.

If evaluation is taken seriously and carried out rigorously as an integral part of the process of innovation, it demands skills, knowledge and a willingness to face up to the consequences of the evidence. In one sense it adds to the burden of innovating since it requires its own resources which includes time, effort, energy and materials. However, evaluation also has its reward: producing innovation that has a real impact on the school. Attention to evaluation might lead to a situation in which the mark of an innovative school was not the number of innovations it adopted but rather the extent to which it undertook the evaluation of new ideas and practices and retained only those for which there was sufficient positive evidence.

Chapter 8

In Conclusion

In recent years the notion of accountability in relation to education has become more prominent (Sockett, 1980; Becher *et al.*, 1981; Lacey and Lawton, 1981). It is not so much that accountability is a new idea, since those involved in education have always been accountable to someone, but rather that the nature and scope of accountability are now given more weight than previously. Of all the aspects of their work for which teachers are held to be accountable, perhaps none is likely to give rise to more searching questions and strong feelings than innovation.

To be accountable is to be bound to give account of something or to be responsible for things to persons. Accountability in education is frequently discussed in terms of those inside the school being responsible for and having to give an account of what happens there to those outside who have a legitimate interest. However, those inside the school are also accountable to each other for what they do. This is particularly significant in relation to innovation since innovation is often very demanding of resources and may require a high proportion of those available. It is also important that innovations are consistent with the overall purposes of the school and innovating individuals or groups have a responsibility to their colleagues to ensure that this is the case. Moreover, one innovation can often require another and may have school-wide implications and so to see an innovation in isolation from the total situation in which it is to occur and as the responsibility of only the innovating individual or group is shortsighted and may lead to problems.

In order to give an account of an innovation a full, rigorous and widely based evaluation is required. This will enable balanced judgements to be made about the success of the innovation and provide evidence on which to base decisions about its future. Evaluation can provide the evidence to justify the innovation, both inside and outside the school, and it can also reveal the weaknesses of innovations introduced as a result of blind belief, a strong personality, or coercion. The difficulties of evaluation have been recognised and the problem of teachers passing judgements on their own efforts has been highlighted. However, eventually, if not initially, an innovation will have to be justified on rational grounds. Accountability will require more than blind belief in untested hypotheses and in the end teachers have to convince others that their innovation is worthwhile.

The headteacher is legally accountable for the curriculum and the efficient running of the school and his particular role in relation to innovation has been discussed. While recognising the ultimate responsibility of the headteacher, there have been demands recently for a greater involvement of teachers in decision-making and in some schools these demands have been met to varying degrees.

Innovation has been shown to be a complex and difficult activity which demands a considerable range of knowledge and skills. This alone, regardless of any other reasons for teacher participation, suggests that wide involvement of teachers is necessary, since all the knowledge and skills are unlikely to be present in a single person. If a team approach to innovation is adopted, it may be asked what special part the headteacher or principal has to play in the team. His position is a difficult one because he carries the ultimate legal responsibility for the curriculum. While he cannot, and some would argue should not, carry out all the tasks associated with the management of innovation, it would be reasonable for his teachers (and governors or managers) to expect him to have sufficient knowledge and expertise to undertake certain leadership roles.

The headteacher is in the best position to have an overall picture of what has to be done and one of his particular leadership tasks is to work out a plan for the management of an innovation that is internally consistent. He should have sufficient knowledge of the theories of curriculum development and innovation and enough practical experience to enable him to undertake this task. However, perhaps a major particular function is to guide and teach his staff. Teachers should be able to expect their headteacher to have sufficient knowledge and experience in the management of innovation to offer them the kind of guidance that will ensure that their efforts are well directed. They should also be able to expect that they can learn about innovating from him. His function as a teacher of teachers is an extremely important one, particularly where the teachers are young or inexperienced, or where an innovation is complex or departs significantly from previous practice. To have a headteacher who displays his knowledge of innovation and who imparts this to his staff will give them increased confidence as well as greater competence to bring about the innovation. The literature has suggested that it is frequently the headteacher who introduces innovations into his school; it is irresponsible of him to do this with insufficient knowledge to see them through to successful implementation. The increasing number of in-service courses in education management is a recognition of this fact.

Although the headteacher may have the overall responsibility and within this may perform specific leadership roles, individual teachers or groups of teachers may also have responsibilities and perform other leadership roles at different stages or for specific tasks. Teachers with expert knowledge or skills can exercise a leadership function as they use their knowledge or skills to help colleagues and to further the progress of the innovation. To be involved in the management of innovation at levels other than the classroom may bring additional work for teachers. However, certain rewards are possible in return for the additional work. There is the possibility of having an influence beyond one's own classroom and the satisfaction of contributing to the successful development and implementation of an innovation. These are intangible rewards whereas the burden of additional work is a reality. There has been considerable discussion in recent years about the desirability of greater involvement of teachers in decision-making and management activities. The responsibilities associated with greater involvement should not be overlooked.

The range of knowledge and expertise necessary for successful innovation has been discussed. This is unlikely to be acquired solely from personal experience. The role of the head as a teacher of teachers has been mentioned but in some cases this may be insufficient and in others unavailable. In-service education can be helpful in relation to general principles of innovation and curriculum development while the use of outside consultants can also contribute to teacher education as well as providing help with a particular innovation. Reading the available relevant literature is another form of teacher education – one which, unfortunately, has been much neglected in the past. Teachers, as well as headteachers, need to be able to demonstrate that they have the knowledge and abilities to plan and manage innovations successfully and to justify the introduction of these innovations. If they are not able to do so there is always the danger that these activities might be undertaken by agencies outside the school. In these circumstances, teachers would then become no more than technicians carrying out the ideas of others, with headteachers acting as administrators.

The need for improvement in education is recognised. If education is to improve and to be sensitive to changes in society, there will be a need for innovation. Education in the future is likely to be more sophisticated and expectations are likely to be higher, and in order to cope with this teachers will need to be more expert and insightful in taking appropriate decisions and actions when it comes to innovations. It is hoped that this book will help them to respond in a professional manner.

This book has a theoretical stance and yet it is well known that there is a tendency among many teachers to disregard theory. In the field of education, theories that have no practical application serve no useful purpose, but equally practice that is not based on theory is likely to be ineffective in the long term. The theories presented in this book are perhaps best described as emergent and they need to be tested in the field. Teachers have an important role to play here: they are in the best position to apply the theories so as to test and verify them. They can then be modified or rejected, whichever is appropriate. In addition, teachers who are actively involved in innovating are well placed to generate new theories of innovation. Such testing and generating of theory are further areas for development of teachers' professionalism.

References

Adams, R. S., and Biddle, B. J. (1970), *Realities of Teaching* (New York: Holt, Rinehart & Winston).

Argyle, M. (1967), 'The social psychology of social change', in *Social Theory and Economic Change*, ed. T. Burns and S. B. Saul (London: Tavistock).

Argyris, C. (1967), 'To-day's problems with to-morrow's organizations', *Journal of Management Studies*, vol. 4, no. 1.

Auld, R. (1976), *The William Tyndale Junior and Infants School*, report of the public inquiry (London: Inner London Education Authority).

Barker Lunn, J. C. (1970), *Streaming in the Primary School* (Slough: National Foundation for Educational Research).

Barnes, L. B. (1967), 'Organizational change and field experimental methods', in *Methods of Organizational Research*, ed. V. H. Vroom (Pittsburgh, Pa: University of Pittsburgh Press).

Barnett, H. G. (1953), *Innovation: The Basis of Cultural Change* (New York: McGraw-Hill).

Bealing, D. (1972), 'The organisation of junior classrooms', *Educational Research*, vol. 14, no. 3.

Becher, T., Eraut, M., and Knight, J. (1981), *Policies for Educational Accountability* (London: Heinemann).

Becher, T., and Maclure, S. (1978), *The Politics of Curriculum Change* (London: Hutchinson).

Belasco, J. A., and Alutto, J. A. (1975), 'Decisional participation and teacher satisfaction', in *Management in Education Reader I: The Management of Organisations and Individuals*, ed. V. P. Houghton, G. A. R. McHugh and C. Morgan (London: Ward Lock/Open University).

Bell, L. A. (1979), 'A discussion of some of the implications of using consultants in schools', *British Educational Research Journal*, vol. 5, no. 1.

Bennis, W. G. (1963), 'A new role for the behavioral sciences: effecting organizational change', *Administrative Science Quarterly*, vol. 8.

Bennis, W. G. (1966), *Changing Organizations* (New York: McGraw-Hill).

Berg, L. (1968), *Risinghill: Death of a Comprehensive School* (Harmondsworth: Penguin).

Bernbaum, G. (1976), 'The role of the head', in *The Role of the Head*, ed. R. S. Peters (London: Routledge & Kegan Paul).

Brickell, H. M. (1961), *Organizing New York State for Educational Change* (Albany, NY: New York State University).

Brickell, H. M. (1964), 'State organization for educational change: a case study and a proposal', in *Innovation in Education*, ed. M. B. Miles (New York: Teachers College Press).

Brown, M. R. (1971), 'Some strategies used in primary schools for initiating and implementing change', unpublished M.Ed. thesis, University of Manchester.

Carlson, R. O. (1964), 'School superintendents and the adoption of modern math: a social structure profile', in *Innovation in Education*, ed. M. B. Miles (New York: Teachers College Press).

Carlson, R. O. (1965), 'Barriers to change in public schools', in *Change Processes in the Public Schools*, ed. R. O. Carlson (Eugene, Oreg.: Center for the Advanced Study of Educational Administration).

CERI (1969), *The Management of Innovation in Education* (Paris: Organisation for Economic Co-operation and Development).

CERI (1973), *Case Studies of Educational Innovation: IV Strategies for Innovation in Education* (Paris: Organisation for Economic Co-operation and Development).

Chin, R., and Benne, K. D. (1976), 'General strategies for effecting changes in human systems', in *The Planning of Change*, 3rd edn, ed. W. G. Bennis, K. D. Benne, R. Chin and K. E. Corey (New York: Holt, Rinehart & Winston).

Coch, L., and French, J. R. P. (1948), 'Overcoming resistance to change', *Human Relations*, vol. 1.

Coombs, P. H. (1968), *The World Educational Crisis* (New York: Oxford University Press).

Dahllöf, U. S. (1970–71), 'Curriculum process analysis and comparative evaluation of school systems', *Paedagogica Europaea*, vol. 6.

DES (1978), *Making INSET Work* (London: HMSO).

Dickinson, N. B. (1975), 'The headteacher as innovator: a study of an English school district', in *Case Studies in Curriculum Change*, ed. W. A. Reid and D. F. Walker (London: Routledge & Kegan Paul).

Eggleston, J. F., Galton, M. J., and Jones, M. (1976), *Processes and Products of Science Teaching* (London: Macmillan).

Elliott, J., and Adelman, C. (1974), *Innovation in Teaching and Action Research: An Interim Report of the Ford Teaching Project* (Norwich: Centre for Applied Research in Education, University of East Anglia).

Evans, P., and Groarke, M. (1975), 'An exercise in managing curriculum development in a primary school' in *Aims, Influence and Change in the Primary School Curriculum*, ed. P. H. Taylor (Slough: National Foundation for Educational Research).

French, J. R. P., Israel, J., and Dagfinn, A. (1960), 'An experiment in participation in a Norwegian factory: dimensions of decison making', *Human Relations*, vol. 13, no. 1.

Gardner, G. (1977), 'Workers' participation: a critical evaluation of Coch and French', *Human Relations*, vol. 30, no. 12.

Gretton, J., and Jackson, M. (1976), *William Tyndale: Collapse of a School or a System?* (London: Allen & Unwin).

Griffiths, D. E. (1964), 'Administrative theory and change in organizations', in *Innovation in Education*, ed. M. B. Miles (New York: Teachers College Press).

Gross, N., Giacquinta, J. B., and Bernstein, M. (1971), *Implementing Organizational Innovations* (New York: Harper & Row).

Guba, E. G. (1968), 'The process of educational innovation', in *Educational Change: The Reality and the Promise*, ed. R. R. Goulet (New York: Citation Press).

Guskin, A. (1969), 'The individual: internal processes and characteristics which inhibit and facilitate knowledge utilization', in *Planning for Innovation Through Dissemination and Utilization of Knowledge*, ed. R. G. Havelock

(Ann Arbor, Mich.: Center for Research on Utilization of Scientific Knowledge).

Halpin, A. W. (1966), *Theory and Research in Administration* (New York: Macmillan).

Halpin, A. W. (1967), 'Change and organizational climate', *Journal of Educational Administration*, vol. 5, no. 1.

Hamilton, D. (1975), 'Handling innovation in the classroom: two Scottish examples', in *Case Studies in Curriculum Change*, ed. W. A. Reid and D. F. Walker (London: Routledge & Kegan Paul).

Havelock, R. G. (ed.) (1969), *Planning for Innovation Through Dissemination and Utilization of Knowledge* (Ann Arbor, Mich.: Center for Research on Utilization of Scientific Knowledge).

Havelock, R. G. (1971), 'The utilization of educational research and development', *British Journal of Educational Technology*, vol. 2, no. 2.

Hilfiker, L. R. (1970), 'Factors relating to the innovativeness of school systems', *Journal of Educational Research*, vol. 64, no. 1.

Holt, M. J. (1976), 'Curriculum development at Sheredes School', in *Rational Curriculum Planning*, ed. J. Walton and J. Welton (London: Ward Lock).

Hoyle, E. (1969), 'How does the curriculum change?', *Journal of Curriculum Studies*, vols 1, 2 and 3.

Hoyle, E. (1970), 'Planned organisational change in education', *Research in Education*, vol. 3.

Hoyle, E. (1974), 'Innovation and the social organisation of the school', in *Creativity of the School*, CERI Technical Report No. 1 (Paris: Organisation for Economic Co-operation and Development).

Hoyles, E. (1968), 'The head as innovator', in *Headship in the 1970s*, ed. B. Allen (Oxford: Blackwell).

Hughes, L. W. (1968), 'Organizational climate – another dimension to the process of innovation?', *Educational Administrative Quarterly*, vol. 3.

Hughes, M. G. (1976), 'The professional-as-administrator: the case of the secondary school head', in *The Role of the Head*, ed. R. S. Peters (London: Routledge & Kegan Paul).

Jackson, P. W. (1968), *Life in Classrooms* (London: Holt, Rinehart & Winston).

Johns, E. A. (1973), *The Sociology of Organizational Change* (Oxford: Pergamon).

Klein, D. (1976), 'Some notes on the dynamics of resistance to change: the defender role', in *Concepts for Social Change*, ed. G. Watson (Washington, DC: National Training Laboratories, NEA).

Kubie, L. S. (1958), *Neurotic Distortion of the Creative Process*, Porter Lecture Series No. 22 (Lawrence, Kans.: University of Kansas Press).

Lacey, C., and Lawton, D. (eds) (1981), *Issues in Evaluation and Accountability* (London: Methuen).

Leavitt, H. J. (1965), 'Applied organizational change in industry: structural, technological and humanistic approaches', in *Handbook of Organizations*, ed. J. A. March (Chicago: Rand McNally).

Lippitt, R., Watson, J., and Westley, B. (1958), *The Dynamics of Planned Change* (New York: Harcourt, Brace & World).

Lortie, D. C. (1969), 'The balance of control and autonomy in elementary school teaching', in *The Semi-Professions and Their Organization*, ed. A. Etzioni (New York: The Free Press).

MacDonald, B., and Rudduck, J. (1971), 'Curriculum research and development projects: barriers to success', *British Journal of Educational Psychology*, vol. 41.

McGregor, D. (1960), *The Human Side of Enterprise* (New York: McGraw-Hill).

McLaughlin, M. W. (1976), 'Implementation as mutual adaptation: change in classroom organization', *Teachers College Record*, vol. 77, no. 3.

Maclure, S. (1973), *Styles of Curriculum Development* (Paris: Organisation for Economic Co-operation and Development).

Marklund, S. (1972), *The New Role of the Teacher in Swedish Innovative Schools* (Paris: Organisation for Economic Co-operation and Development).

Mather, D. R. (1970), 'The human element in curriculum change', *Journal of Curriculum Studies*, vol. 2, no. 1.

Miles, M. B. (1964a), 'Educational innovation: the nature of the problem', in *Innovation in Education*, ed. M. B. Miles (New York: Teachers College Press).

Miles, M. B. (1964b), 'On temporary systems', in *Innovation in Education*, ed. M. B. Miles (New York: Teachers College Press).

Miles, M. B. (1964c), 'Innovation in education: some generalizations', in *Innovation in Education*, ed. M. B. Miles (New York: Teachers College Press).

Miles, M. B. (1965), 'Planned change and organizational health: figure and ground', in *Change Processes in the Public Schools*, ed. R. O. Carlson (Eugene, Oreg.: University of Oregon Press).

Miller, R. I. (1967), 'An overview of educational change', in *Perspectives on Educational Change*, ed. R. I. Miller (New York: Appleton-Century-Crofts).

Mitchell, P. (1972), 'Social science in the secondary school curriculum', *Journal of Curriculum Studies*, vol. 4, no. 2.

Mort, P. R. (1964), 'Studies in educational innovation from the Institute of Educational Research: an overview', in *Innovation in Education*, ed. M. B. Miles (New York: Teachers College Press).

Moss, D. J. (1977), 'Developing the curriculum in a new comprehensive school', in *Control of the Curriculum*, ed. R. Glatter (London: University of London Institute of Education).

Musgrove, F. (1973), 'The curriculum for a world of change', in *The Curriculum: Research, Innovation and Change*, ed. P. H. Taylor and J. Walton (London: Ward Lock).

Musgrove, F., and Taylor, P. H. (1969), *Society and the Teacher's Role* (London: Routledge & Kegan Paul).

Nevermann, K. (1974), 'The relationship of the formal organization of, and informal grouping within, a school to its creativity', in *Creativity of the School*, CERI Technical Report No. 1 (Paris: Organisation for Economic Co-operation and Development).

Nicholls, A. (1979), 'The planning and implementation of an educational innovation: a case study', unpublished PhD thesis, The Queen's University of Belfast.

Nicholls, A., and Nicholls, S. H. (1978), *Developing a Curriculum: A Practical Guide*, 2nd edn (London: Allen & Unwin).

Nicholls, S. H., and Nicholls, A. (1975), *Creative Teaching* (London: Allen & Unwin).

Nisbet, J. (1974), 'Innovation – bandwagon or hearse?' (The Frank Tate Memorial Lecture), in *Curriculum Innovation*, ed. A. Harris, M. Lawn and W. Prescott (London: Croom Helm).

Noel, G. (1974), 'The factors (positive or negative) in educational innovation at secondary level in the French system', in *Creativity of the School*, CERI Technical Report No. 1 (Paris: Organisation for Economic Co-operation and Development).

Owen, J. G. (1973), *The Management of Curriculum Development* (Cambridge: Cambridge University Press).

Owens, R. G. (1970), *Organizational Behavior in Schools* (Englewood Cliffs, NJ: Prentice Hall).

Pellegrin, R. J. (1967), *An Analysis of Sources and Processes of Innovation in Education* (Eugene, Oreg.: Center for the Advanced Study of Educational Administration, University of Oregon).

Peters, R. S. (1966), *Ethics and Education* (London: Allen & Unwin).

Prosser, P. J. (1976), 'Cranbourne Middle School', in *Rational Curriculum Planning*, ed. J. Walton and J. Welton (London: Ward Lock).

Richardson, E. (1967), *The Environment of Learning* (London: Nelson).

Richardson, E. (1975), *Authority and Organization in the Secondary School* (London: Macmillan).

Rogers, E. M. (1962), *Diffusion of Innovations* (New York: The Free Press).

Rogers, E. M. (1965), 'What are innovators like?', in *Change Processes in the Public Schools*, ed. R. O. Carlson (Eugene, Oreg.: Center for the Advanced Study of Educational Administration).

Rogers, E. M., and Shoemaker, F. F. (1971), *Communication of Innovations: A Cross Cultural Approach*, 2nd edn (New York: The Free Press).

Ross, D. H. (1958), *Administration for Adaptability* (New York: Metropolitan School Study Council).

Rubin, L. J. (1968), 'Installing an innovation', in *Educational Change: The Reality and the Promise*, ed. R. R. Goulet (New York: Citation Press).

Schmuck, R. A. (1974), 'Interventions for strengthening the school's creativity', in *Creativity of the School*, CERI Technical Report No. 1 (Paris: Organisation for Economic Co-operation and Development).

Schmuck, R. A., and Miles, M. B. (1971), *Organizational Development in Schools* (Palo Alto, Calif.: National Press).

Schon, D. A. (1971), *Beyond the Stable State* (London: Temple Smith).

Schools Council (1968), *Young School Leavers. Enquiry I* (London: HMSO).

Sharp, R., and Green, A. (1975), *Education and Social Control* (London: Routledge & Kegan Paul).

Shipman, M. (1974), *Inside a Curriculum Project* (London: Methuen).

Smith, L. M., and Keith, P. M. (1971), *Anatomy of Educational Innovation: An Organizational Analysis of an Elementary School* (New York: Wiley).

Sockett, H. (ed.) (1980), *Accountability in the English Education System* (London: Hodder & Stoughton).

Stenhouse, L. (1975), *An Introduction to Curriculum Research and Development* (London: Heinemann).

Stinchcombe, A. L. (1965), 'Social Structure and organizations', in *Handbook of Organizations*, ed. J. A. March (Chicago: Rand McNally).

Strauss, G. (1963), 'Some notes on power equalization', in Leavitt, H. D. (ed), *The Social Science of Organizations* (Englewood Cliffs, NJ: Prentice-Hall).

Tomlinson, J. (1978), address at the Convocation of the Schools Council, reported in the *Daily Telegraph*, 15 November, p. 10.

Trow, M. (1970), 'Methodological problems in the evaluation of innovations', in *The Evaluation of Instruction*, ed. M. G. Wittrock and D. E. Wiley (New York: Holt, Rinehart & Winston).

Trump, J. L. (1967), 'Influencing change at the secondary level', in *Perspectives on Educational Change*, ed. R. I. Miller (New York: Appleton-Century-Crofts).

Urwick, L. (1963), *The Elements of Administration* (London: Pitman).

Walton, J., and Welton, J. (1976), *Rational Curriculum Planning* (London: Ward Lock).

Watson, G. (1967), 'Toward a conceptual architecture of a self-renewing school system', in *Concepts for Social Change*, ed. G. Watson (Washington, DC: National Training Laboratories, NEA).

Wilson, J. Q. (1966), 'Innovation in organizations: notes toward a theory', in *Approaches to Organizational Design* (Pittsburgh, Pa: University of Pittsburgh Press).

Young, M. (1965), *Innovation and Research in Education* (London: Routledge & Kegan Paul).

Index